A Veldt Ven

Bertram Mitford

Alpha Editions

This edition published in 2024

ISBN : 9789362921635

Design and Setting By
Alpha Editions
www.alphaedis.com
Email - info@alphaedis.com

Contents

Chapter One.

A Voyage of Discovery.

I had not a friend in the world.

My own fault? No doubt. It is usually said so, at any rate, so of course must be true. For I, Kenrick Holt, who do this tale unfold, am not by nature and temperament an expansive animal, rather the reverse, being constitutionally reticent; and, is it not written that the world takes you at your own valuation? Still, I had managed to muddle on through life somehow, and gain a living so far—which was satisfactory, but in an uncongenial and sedentary form of occupation—which was not. Incidentally I owned to the ordinary contingent of acquaintances, but at the period of which I write I had not a friend in the world—only brothers.

Of these, one owned an abominable wife, the other a snug country living, which combination of circumstances may account for the fact that we had rather less to do with each other on the whole than the latest conjunction of club acquaintances. Incidentally, too, I owned relatives, but for ordinary reasons, not material to this narrative, they didn't count.

"Great events from little causes spring" is a truism somewhat shiny at the seams. In the present instance the "little cause" took the form of an invite from the last-mentioned of my two brethren—he who drew comfortable subsidy for shepherding a few rustics in the national creed to wit—to run down and get through a week with him at his vicarage.

I was out of sorts and "hipped," not so much through overwork as through remaining in town too long at a stretch: for, except a day off now and then up the river, I had stuck to my office all through the hot months, and it was now September. In passing, it may be mentioned I held a secretaryship to a not very long floated company; a fairly good berth—as long as it lasted. As long as it lasted! There lay the rub. For I had held two similar berths before!

Well, this invite came in pat. A blow of country air would do me all the good in the world just then. The invite was something of an event, as may be conjectured in the light of certain foregoing remarks; still, that didn't matter. Nothing did—according to my then philosophy—except lack of the needful, and an abominable noise when one wanted to go to sleep. The first I had experienced more than once, the second I was destined to—and notably if I accepted the invite. However, that didn't weigh. The only thing that remained was to pack up and send a wire.

I had packed, and found out a convenient train. But the first thing in the morning brought a counter-wire—

"Sorry must put you off dick and bertha got scarlatina holt."

Here was a nuisance—the said Dick and Bertha being among the certain arch-contributors in prospective to the second of the things that matter in life, as referred to above. Yes, it was a nuisance. I was all ready to start, and the weather was perfect; just that soft, golden, hazy kind of September weather that is exquisite in the country, and here was I, doomed to the reek of asphalt and wood paving once more, just as I was rejoicing in the prospect of a week of emancipation therefrom. Well, I would go somewhere, but it wasn't the same thing, for I am not partial to solitary jaunts, albeit in most matters self-concentrated. At any rate, I would not go back to work.

I strolled round to the club, thinking out an objective the while. There were few *habitués* there, but a sprinkling of strangers, for we were housing another kindred institution pending its summer cleaning. Among these was a man I knew, and as we got talking over our "split" I found he was in the same predicament as myself.

"Don't know where to go?" he said. "I'll tell you. There's a jolly little place on the Dorsetshire coast—Whiddlecombe Regis—right out of the public beat, only known to a few, and they always go back there. Jolly pretty country, first-rate bathing, and not bad sea fishing. Let's run down together for a week or so. We can capture a train from Waterloo at a decent hour to-morrow. Waiter, just fetch me the ABC, will you?"

The ABC was fetched, and we put our heads together over it, and in the result the following afternoon saw us deposited—after a five-mile coach ride from the nearest station—in front of the principal inn at Whiddlecombe Regis.

It was a delightfully picturesque and retired place, with its one long steep street, and flat massive church tower; and seemed to deserve all the encomium which Bindley had bestowed upon it. It nestled snugly in its own bay, which was guarded by bold headlands, all crimson and gold with heather and gorse, shooting out into the sparkling blue of a summer sea. Not a cloud was in the sky, and against the soft haze in the offing a trail of smoke here and there marked out the flight of a passing steamer.

Our "decent train from Waterloo" had proved to be a dismally early one, consequently we found ourselves at our destination at an early hour of the afternoon. So after we had lunched—plainly but exceedingly well—I suggested we should go down to the beach and take on a good pull if there was a light boat to be had, and a sail if there was not.

But Bindley was not an ideal travelling companion; I had found that out in more than one trifling particular on the way down. Nor did he now jump at my suggestion with the alacrity it deserved—or at any rate which I thought it did. He made various objections. It was too hot—and so forth. He felt more like taking it easy. What was the good in coming away for a rest if one began by grinding one's soul out? he said.

However, I was bursting with long-pent-up energy. The glorious open air, after the reek and fogginess of London had already begun to put new life into me, and the smooth blue of the sea and its fresh salt whiff invited its exploration. So I left Bindley to laze in peace and took my way down to the beach. For a moment I had felt inclined to fall in with his idea, or at any rate to wait an hour or two until he felt inclined to fall in with mine, but the feeling passed. How little I knew what the next twelve hours or so were destined to bring forth!

The beach at Whiddlecombe Regis held everything in common with the beach at half a hundred similar places. There were the same fishing boats and the same whiff thereof—some with their brown sails up and drying, and two or three of their blue jerseyed owners doing odd jobs about them; others alone and deserted, with nets hung over the side to dry. Children were paddling in the little sparkling rims of froth left by each ripple of the tide, and under the redolent shelter of the boats aforesaid their nurses and governesses, seated beneath sunshades, gossipped, or looked up from the *Family Herald* to inspect the passing male stranger and grumble at the heat.

"Boat, sir?"

The hail, proceeded from a weather-beaten seafarer. I was beyond the fishing craft by now, and in front lay, drawn up on the beach, a dozen or so of rowing boats and—marvellous to relate—among them one, light and an outrigger.

"Well, I feel like an hour's pull," I answered. "This one will do."

The salt looked out seaward a moment. Then he said—

"Well, sir, she be only good in smooth water, and it's that now. Be you much in the way of boats, sir?"

"Rather," I answered readily, for I fancied myself in the sculling line, it being one of my favourite forms of recreation. And I suppose I looked my words, for my amphibious friend ran the pair-oar down into the water without more ado.

Though not a skiff, the craft was light and well built, and in a very few moments I was sending her over the smooth waters of the bay at a pace which should soon render the village of Whiddlecombe Regis a mere blur against a wall of green hillside and crimson-clad down—and that without any effort. The exhilaration of it was glorious—the swift easy glide, the free open sea, the cloudless blue sky above, and the racing headlands. Beyond these other promontories appeared; only to be merged in their turn into the spreading extent of the fast-receding coastline. The boat went beautifully. I had got her over half a dozen miles in no time. I would make it a round dozen straight out; then back—and get in at dusk, in nice time for dinner.

What an ass Bindley was to come down to a place like this merely for the fun of going to sleep, I thought, as I skimmed onwards; and then it occurred to me that as this was the only craft of the kind on the beach, I should have missed the splendid exhilaration afforded by my present exercise, as she was certainly not built to carry two, and I had thoughts of hiring her for the time I should be down here, so as to ensure always being able to take her out when wanted.

I had, as near as could be judged by time, about accomplished my prescribed dozen miles, and was pulling the boat round to return, when in spite of the exercise I felt chilly. Then as I faced out to seaward and perceived the cause I felt chillier still—and with reason.

Fog.

Creeping up swiftly, insidiously, like a dark curtain over the sea it was already upon me. Heavens! how I pulled. But pull I never so lustily, send the light craft foaming through the water as I was doing, the dread enemy was swifter still—and all too subtle. Already the coastline was half blotted out, and the remainder blurred and indistinct, but up-Channel the sea was still clear. Well, by holding a straight course now, and keeping what little wind there was upon my right ear, I could still fetch the land even if I did not soon run into clear weather again.

But the smother deepened, lying thick upon the surface. Already the air seemed darkening, and now a distance of half a dozen yards on either hand was all that was visible—sometimes not as much.

Was it demoralisation evoked by this sudden blotting out of the world around, as I found myself alone in the dark vastness of this spectral silence?—for now I felt tired and was obliged to rest on my sculls more than once. And again and again, though hot and perspiring, I shivered.

Now through the silence came the whooping of a steamer's siren. Another, further out, answered in ghostly hoot. Heavens! what did this mean? Had I, while resting, been insidiously turned round and was now sculling my utmost out into mid-Channel—and—right into the path of passing shipping? And with the thought it occurred to me that no sound of the shore—the striking of a church clock or the bark of a dog, for instance, reached my ears. The thought was an uncomfortable one—almost appalling. One thing was clear. Further rowing was of no use at all.

Again rose the hoot of that spectral foghorn, and as it ceased I lifted up my voice and shouted like mad. But the steamer was probably not near enough for those on board of her to hear my yell, and from the repetition of the sound she seemed to be passing.

It was now almost dark. Shivering violently, I put on my coat and waistcoat—which I had thrown off when beginning my pull—but they were light summer flannels and of small protection—and looked the situation in the face. Here was I, in a cockleshell of a craft, which even the smallest rising of the sea would inevitably swamp, shut in by thick impenetrable fog anywhere out towards mid-Channel, and drifting Heaven knew where, with nothing to eat, nothing to drink, and a long night before me to do it in. I might be picked up, but it was even more likely I might be run down, and with the thought I seemed to see a black, towering cut-water rush foaming from the oily smother, to crash into my little craft and bear me down drowning and battered beneath the grim iron keel.

Time went by; it must have been hours—to me it seemed years. In the overwhelming unearthly blackness of the fog I sat and shivered, a prey to the most unutterably helpless feeling. If it were only daylight, and the fog would lift, I should be picked up in no time in so congested a waterway as the Channel was at this point. But such a consideration now only served to enhance the horror of the position, for it wanted hours and hours to daylight, and here I was, with no means of showing a light except a matchbox containing some dozen and a half of wax vestas, and right in the way of anything that came along. That was an idea anyhow. I might light a pipe. The glow, tiny as it was, might attract notice in the dark. But though a greater smoker than the average I am not one of those who can enjoy tobacco on an empty stomach, and the latter condition being all there, I soon had to desist, and think of the cosy dinner we should now long since have been sitting down to, Bindley and I, in the snug inn at Whiddlecombe Regis; which, whether it lay north, south, east or west of me at that moment, Heaven only knew.

It may be guessed I had expended a good deal of lung power in periodical shouting. I had heard fog-horns whooping from time to time, but more or less distant, and once I had heard the powerful beat of a propeller and the rush of a great liner, quite near by. But as Fate would have it, at that critical point I had shouted myself well-nigh voiceless, and the clank and clatter on board and the wash of her way must have drowned my feeble attempts, for she passed on, and presently a succession of waves furrowed up by her passage caused my little cockleshell to dance in the most lively fashion. Thus I was left alone in the blackness once more, sick and faint with hunger, and my teeth chattering with the cold, to such an extent that it seemed to me the very noise they made ought in itself to attract the attention of passing craft.

After that I seemed to fall into a state of semi-somnolence for a time, out of which I was roused by the motion of the boat. I awoke with a start. There was a freshening in the air, as though a breeze were springing up; and indeed such was the case. The fog, too, had lifted, for I could see stars. But the momentary exultation evoked by this idea subsided in a new alarm. The sea was getting up, and I needed not a reminder of the old salt from whom I had hired the boat that the latter was only good for smooth water. Here was a new peril, and a very real one. And there was a decidedly "open sea" kind of whiff about the freshening breeze.

I pulled the boat round so as to keep her head to the waves, which seemed to be increasing every moment. Their splash wetted me, rendering the cold more biting than ever, and then—a strange roaring sound bellowed in my ears. A huge green eye shot forward in the darkness, and a tall dark mass towered foaming above me. At that moment I opened my mouth and emitted the most awful yell that ever proceeded from human throat. Then came the crash—as I knew it would. I seemed to be shot forward into space, then dragged through leagues of cold and rushing waters, while gripping something hard and resisting as though life depended on it. Then another shock, and I knew no more.

Chapter Two.

A Waif.

"Seems to be coming to, don't he?"

"Not quite. Better leave him alone a bit longer."

Was I dead, and were these voices of another world? Hardly. They had a homely and British intonation which savoured too much of this one. Then I grew confused, and dozed off again.

Was I dreaming, or where was I? shaped out the next thought as I heard the voices again. Lying with closed eyes, returning consciousness began to assert itself. A certain heaving movement, which could be produced by nothing else than a ship at sea, made itself felt—a movement not unknown to me, for I had made a voyage to Australia and back earlier in my hitherto uneventful career—and a pounding, vibrating sound, which jarred somewhat roughly upon my awakened nerves, told that the vessel was a steamship. Opening my eyes drowsily, I saw that I was lying in a bunk, and the fresh air blowing in through an open skylight was breezy and salt. There was no mistaking my present quarters. I was in a ship's cuddy. A table, covered with a faded cloth of many colours, stood in the middle of the room, and the slant of an apparently useless pillar running from floor to ceiling, and through the same, could only be that of a mast.

"Feeling better now, sir?"

Two men had glided into the room and were watching me. One was tall, slim, and well made, with a clear-cut face and dark pointed beard, the other red and broad and burly; and when they spoke I recognised the voices I had heard before.

"Yes, thanks. At least I think so," I answered faintly.

"Better give him a tot of rum. That'll bring him to," said the broad red man, in a voice that rumbled.

"Not much. Grog on top of that whack on the head he got would be the death of him. Oh, steward! tell the doctor to send along that broth," he called out to some one outside.

"Where am I?" was my next and obvious question.

"Board the *Kittiwake*, bound for East London. Cargo, iron rails," answered the broad red man.

"Let's see. You ran me down, didn't you?" I said confusedly.

"Run you down? Well, sonny, you lurched your ironclad against our bows in a way that was reckless. And you warn't carrying no lights neither, which is clean contrary to Board o' Trade regulations, and dangerous to shippin'."

"What a narrow squeak I must have had. Are you the captain?"

"No, sir. This here's the captain, Captain John Morrissey," and he turned to the good-looking, dark-bearded man, whom at first I had taken for the ship's surgeon.

"Narrow squeak's hardly the word for it, Mr Holt," said this man in a pleasant voice. "It's more of a miracle than I've seen in all my experience of sea-going. Ah, I see the doctor has sent you your broth; you'd better take it, and I wouldn't talk too much just yet, if I were you."

"You carry a doctor, then. Are you a liner?"

Both laughed at this.

"No, no, Mr Holt," answered the captain. "Doctor's a seafaring term for the ship's cook, and I believe in this instance you'll find his prescriptions do you more good than those of the real medico."

I sipped the broth, and felt better; but still had a very confused, not to say achy, feeling about the head, and again began to feel drowsy.

"I suppose I'll be all right by the time we get in," I said. "Right enough to land, shan't I?"

The broad red man rumbled out a deep guffaw. The captain's face took on a strange look—comical and warning at the same time.

"You'll be all right long before we get in, Mr Holt," he said. "Now, if you take my advice, you'll go to sleep again."

I did take it, and I must have slept for a long time. Once or twice I half woke, and it seemed to be night, for all was dark save for a faint light coming in through the closed portholes, and the lulling rocking movement and swish of the water soon sent me off again. Even the throb of the propeller was soothing in its regularity.

"You've had a good sleep, sir. Feel better this morning, sir?"

It was broad daylight, and the motion of the ship had changed to a very decided roll. I sat up in my bunk.

"Shall we be in soon, steward?" I asked, recognising that functionary.

"Be in soon? Why, hardly, sir," he answered, looking puzzled. "We don't touch nowhere."

"No, I suppose not. But where are we now?"

"Well into the Bay."

"The Bay! What Bay?"

"Bay o' Biscay, sir," he replied, looking as though he thought the effects of my buffeting had impaired my reasoning faculties.

"Bay of Biscay!" I echoed. "The Channel, you mean. The captain said we were bound for East London."

"So we are, sir, and we're heading there at nine knots an hour. We shan't do so much, though, if this sou'wester keeps up."

An idea struck me, but it was a confused one.

"Steward," I said, sitting bolt upright. "Will you oblige me with a piece of information. Where the devil *is* East London?"

"Eastern end of the Cape Colony, Mr Holt; and a bad port of call, whichever way you take it."

The answer came from the captain, who entered at that moment. The steward went on with his occupation, that of laying the table for breakfast.

"Great Scott!" I cried, as the truth dawned upon me. "But—"

"I see how it stands," said the captain with a smile. "You thought East London meant the East India Docks. I didn't set you right at the time, because you might have got into a state of excitement, and rest was the word just then. Now I think you are fairly on your legs again."

"But—botheration! I don't want to take a voyage to the Cape. I suppose you can put me ashore somewhere, so I can get back."

"I'm afraid not. We don't touch anywhere. But I think even the voyage is the lesser evil of the two. Better than lying at the bottom of the Channel, I mean."

"Well, certainly. Don't think me ungrateful, Captain Morrissey; but this will mean a lot to me. I shall lose my berth, for one thing."

"Even that isn't worse than losing your life, and you had a narrow squeak of that. By the way, were you sculling across the Channel for a bet?"

"Haw, haw, haw!" rumbled the broad red man, who had rolled in in time to catch this question.

I joined in the laugh, and told them how I came to be found in such a precarious plight. Then I learned how my rescue had been effected, and indeed miraculous hardly seemed the word for it. But that the steamer was going dead slow in the fog, and I had clung to her straight stern with the grip of death, I should have been crushed down beneath her and cut to pieces by the propeller. Even then they had hauled me on board with difficulty. The boat, of course, had been knocked to matchwood.

"You had a gold watch and chain upon you, a pocket-book, and some money?" said the captain. "How much was there?"

"Let me see; five pounds and some change. I forget how much."

The captain disappeared through a door, and immediately re-entered.

"Count that," he said.

I picked up a five-pound note, two sovereigns, and some silver change.

"Seven pounds, nine and a halfpenny," I said. "Yes, that's about what it was."

"That's all right. I took care of it for you. Here's your watch and chain. I ventured to open the pocket-book to find out your identity. Now, if you'll take my advice you'll get up and join us at breakfast."

I took it, and soon the captain and I and the broad red man, who was the chief mate, and rejoiced in the name of Chadwick, were seated at table, and I don't know that grilled chops and mashed potato—for the fresh meat supply had not yet run out—ever tasted better. The while we discussed the situation.

"The nearest point I could land you at would be the Canaries," the captain was saying, "and I daren't do that. My owners are deadly particular, and it might be as much as my bunk was worth—and I've got a family to support."

"Well, I haven't," I answered, "so I wouldn't allow you to take any risk of the kind on my account, captain, even if you were willing to. But—what about passing steamers?"

The two sailors looked at each other.

"The fact is," went on the captain, "it's blowing not only fresh, but strong. The glass is dropping in a way that points to the next few days finding us with our hands all full. After that we shan't sight anything much this side of the Cape, and it'll hardly be worth your while to tranship then. I'm afraid you'll have to make up your mind to do the whole passage with us."

I recognised the force of this, and that it was a case of resigning myself to the inevitable. And the thought ran through my mind how strange are the workings of events. But for my brother's invite I should have been safe and snug and humdrum in my City office. But for the cancelling of that invite I should never have found my way to Whiddlecombe Regis, or even have heard of such a place; and now here I was, after a perilous experience, launched upon the high seas, bound for a distant colony, and that without any will of my own in the matter. Well, when I got there, I could always arrange a return passage. I had some means of my own—not enough to keep me without working, unless I chose to live upon what would amount to the wages of an artisan. Therefore there was nothing to cause me serious anxiety, unless it were that my berth would probably be filled up. But, as I have hinted, the tenure of it was somewhat precarious, so some consolation lay that way, and I could doubtless find another. So I reasoned, forgetting that after all we are blind and helpless instruments in the hands of Fate, a lesson which my experience so far might well have reminded me—certainly in total unconsciousness of what stirring experiences, perilous and otherwise, lay between now and when I should once more behold the English coastline.

"You seem a good sailor, at any rate, Mr Holt," said the captain, breaking in upon my meditations.

"Why, I never thought of feeling seasick," I answered. "It didn't occur to me."

"No? Well, you're all right then. If we've done, I would suggest a turn on deck. If we get a bad blow, you may not be able to get there for a while, so better make the most of it now."

Chapter Three.

Southward.

A stirring and lively scene met my gaze as I emerged from the companion-way. A great waste of roaring tumbling seas, their dull green mountainous masses breaking off into foamy crests as they swooped down upon us, only to swing under the keel and roar on afresh in a moving mountain beyond. The sky, a great flying scud which glimpses of sickly sunshine strove here and there to pierce. White gulls hovered and darted, squealing; and, thrown out in a cloud of proud magnificence against the inky sky to the westward, a homeward-bound ship, under a full spread of canvas, was thundering over the boil of billows, dashing the white spray before her in cataracts.

From the poop-deck I could see for the first time what manner of craft I was in. The *Kittiwake* was an iron steamer of just under two thousand tons, brig rigged; and the water was pouring from her forecastle as she dipped her nose into the meeting of the green seas. Some of the hands were running up the foresail to the accompaniment of a shrill nautical chant, and the broad red man, clad in oilskins, had just gone up to relieve the second mate on the bridge. To a landsman's eye, the aspect of the weather quarter looked black and threatening to the last degree, and it hardly needed the captain's warning that a dusty time, which would keep all hands busy, was in front of us.

"You were saying you had no incubus in the matter of family dependent on you, Mr Holt," the captain remarked as we paced the short poop-deck, which was literally, as he put it, fisherman's walk—three steps and overboard. "But I hope you've left no one behind who'll be anxious about you."

"Not a soul," I answered. "I have no friends, only relations, and their only anxiety—at least, on the part of one of two of the nearest—will be as to how soon they can file claims to what little I possess."

The other laughed drily at this, and there was a twinkle of sympathetic fun in his eyes.

"After them, the most anxious person will be the man who let me the boat," I said. "But I can compensate him, with interest, later on."

I thought of Bindley, and how my disappearance might possibly spoil his holiday; but then, I didn't suppose it would. He was one of those men who ought to go about by themselves; in fact, I wondered why he had moved me to join him in this jaunt, seeing that his idea of companionable travelling was to go to sleep most of the time or to read the papers all through dinner. No, he wouldn't mind. On the contrary, it would give him matter to oraculise upon.

The next three days were something to remember, and we spent most of them and the corresponding nights either hove to or going dead slow. I had been through rough weather before, but never such an experience as that, and, to tell the truth, never do I want to again. Black darkness, only qualified by a dim oil lamp—for the captain had insisted on my remaining below—thunderous roaring, crashing and poundings as though the ship were being ground in pieces between two mighty icebergs. And then the inert uncertainty of it! Every upheave seemed to be followed by a downward settling plunge, as though the ship were already on her way to the bottom. The steward and I stole furtive looks at each other from white faces as we moved about, nearly knee-deep in water, and I think the same thought was in both our minds, that each sickening plunge was going to be the last. Seriously, that momentary expectation of death, condemned the while to utter inaction and surrounded by every circumstance of appalling tumult and darkness and horror, is about as unnerving a thing as can find place in any man's experience, and it was long before the recollection of it passed from my mind.

Assuredly, too, I shall never forget the scene that greeted my first appearance on deck, after the subsidence of the storm.

The steamer, which before, though lacking the spick-and-span smartness of a crack liner, was, for a cargo boat, wonderfully clean and ship-shape, now had all the appearance of a wreck. Everything movable on her decks had been swept away. Three out of her four boats were gone, and the green seas came pouring over the main deck, to run off through a great breach in her bulwarks. Crates of poultry and a live sheep alike had disappeared, and she wore the aspect of a woe-begone hulk. However, we had weathered the gale, and the engines had stood out nobly.

The captain and chief mate, too, looked hardly the same men. The former was pale and sallow, and the latter, though still broad, could no longer be described as red. The long spell of sleeplessness and terrible anxiety had told upon them, and the eyes of both were dull and opaque. I did not address them, as they were busily engaged in "shooting the sun," it being the first time that luminary had been available for the purpose since the beginning of the gale.

"Running down the Portuguese coast, and a sight nearer in than we ought to be," said the captain, joining me. "Well, Mr Holt, you've had a new experience, and I'm not sure I haven't myself, for I can hardly call to mind a worse blow, especially with such a cargo, and loaded down as we are. The boat won't rise properly, you see—hasn't a fair chance. Well, we shan't get any more of it, unless we come in for a dusting off the Cape coast."

We ran into lovely weather—day after day of cloudless skies and glassy seas; but the heat on the line was something to remember, and we had none of the luxuries of a first-class passenger ship—no long drinks or iced lager, or cool salads and oranges. Salt provisions and ship biscuit and black tea, with a tot of grog before turning in, constituted our luxurious fare, and the heat had brought out innumerable cockroaches, which did their level best to contribute towards its seasoning. But there were compensations. For instance, I had made up my mind to leave all care and anxiety behind, to throw it off utterly, and trust to luck; and having done this, in spite of drawbacks, I began to enjoy the situation amazingly.

I had long since come to the conclusion that the captain was one of the nicest fellows I had ever met. He was utterly unlike any preconceived and conventional idea of the merchant skipper. He never swore or hustled his crew, or laid down the law, or did any of those things which story has immemorially associated with his cloth. And he was refined and cultured, and could talk well on matters outside his professional experience. He was rather a religious man, too, though he never put it forward, but I frequently saw him reading books of Catholic authorship or compilation, so guessed at his creed. As an Irishman, too, he was quite outside the preconceived type in that he was neither quick-tempered nor impulsive, and in his speech it was difficult to detect anything but the faintest trace of brogue. Chadwick, the first mate, who soon recovered all his original redness, was a rough diamond, whose table manners perhaps might not have been appreciated in the saloon of a first-class liner, yet he was an excellent fellow, and the same held good of the chief engineer. But the second mate, King, I own to disliking intensely. He was a dark-bearded, sallow-faced young man, with a cockney drawl and an infallible manner. He was certainly the most argumentative fellow I have ever met. There was no subject under heaven on which he would not undertake to set us all right. The captain bore with him in good-humouredly contemptuous silence. Chadwick used to sledgehammer him with a growl and a flat contradiction, but it was like sledge-hammering a flea on an eider-down cushion. He hopped up livelier than ever, with a challenge to his superior to prove his contradiction.

One day he had been trying my patience to the very utmost, when duty called him elsewhere. I turned to the chief engineer, who had formed one of the group, with something like relief.

"Upon my word, McBean, that messmate of yours is appropriately named."

"Who? King?"

"Yes."

"And why?"

"Because he 'can do no wrong.'"

- 15 -

"Ay," said the Scot. "And do ye thenk the king can do no wrang?"

I looked at McBean. But the rejoinder was perfectly and innocently serious.

I do not propose to dwell further on the voyage, for it was uneventful, and therefore like a score of other such voyages. But to myself it was very enjoyable, in spite of passing drawbacks, and more so than ever when one night Chadwick pointed out the Agulhas light—very far away, for we had given that perilous coast particularly wide sea room—and I knew that a few days would see us at our destination.

For the said few days we could see the loom of the coast line on our port beam, high, in parts mountainous, but indistinct, for the skipper knew enough of that coast to appreciate the value of sea room. Finally we drew in nearer, and I could make out green stretches sloping upward from the shore and intersected here and there by strips of dark jungle. A dull unceasing roar was borne outward, denoting that the lines of white water lashing this mysterious-looking coast represented heavy surf. Then in the distance there hove in sight a squat lighthouse and the roofs of a few houses.

"There's your land of promise, Holt," said the captain, joining me. "We shall be at anchor by three o'clock. Meanwhile you'd better go down to dinner."

Strange to say, I felt disinclined to do anything of the kind. The voyage was over, and I had a distinct and forlorn feeling that I was about to be literally turned adrift, and I believe at that moment I would have decided to return by the *Kittiwake* even as I had come; but such a course was impossible, for after she had discharged she was to leave for Bombay, in ballast. So I leaned over the side, gazing somewhat resentfully at this fair land, with its infinite range of possibilities, of which at that moment I was hardly thinking at all. For over and above the impending farewells, I was wondering how on earth I was going to get along in a strange land where I knew not a soul, with seven pounds nine and a half penny as my present assets.

Chapter Four.

On a Strange and Distant Shore.

"Well, good-bye, Holt. Wish you every luck if I don't see you again, but I expect I shall if you stop on a day or two at the hotel yonder. I'll be getting a run on shore—when I can."

Thus the captain, and then came Chadwick, and the chief engineer—all wishing me a most hearty good-bye. Even toward the obnoxious King I felt quite affectionately disposed. The crew too were singing out, "Good luck to you, sir."

I could hardly say anything in return, for I felt parting with these excellent fellows and good comrades, whose involuntary guest I had been during four weeks. Then I slid down the rope ladder on to the great surf boat which had been signalled alongside to take me off.

There were other vessels in the roadstead, sailing craft and a white-hulled, red-funnelled coasting steamer of the Castle line. It was a dull, sunless afternoon, which enhanced my depressed and forlorn feeling considerably. The surf boat was one of several that had been discharging cargo from the other shipping, which was stowed away in her hold, leaving room for me in the very small space open at either end. She was worked by a hawser and half a dozen black fellows, and a very rough specimen of a white man, with a great tangled beard, and a stock of profanity both original and extensive.

"Now, mister," sang out this worthy, as I was waving last farewells to those on board, "stow that—and yer bloomin' carcase too, unless yer want yer ruddy nut cracked with the blanked rope. Get down into the bottom of the boat."

The warning, though rough, was all needed, for hardly had I obeyed it, when bang—whigge! the great hawser flew taut like some huge bowstring, just where my head had been a moment before. For a little while I judged it expedient literally to lie low, but when I eventually looked up, it was to behold an immense green wall of water towering aft. It curled and hissed—then broke upon us with a thunderous crash, and for half a minute I didn't know whether we were in the boat or in the sea; and had hardly time to take breath when another followed.

"Hang on, mister, hang on," bellowed the captain, after the first storm of profanity which burst from him had spent itself. "Hang on for all you're worth. There's more coming."

I took his advice. There was a quick gliding movement, an upheave and a bump—and then—crash came one of the mighty rollers as before. Another and another followed, and at length, half drowned, I realised we were in smooth water again, and ventured cautiously to look up.

We were in the mouth of a fine river, banked by high bluffs covered with thick virgin forest. On the left bank lay a township of sorts, and the lighthouse I had seen. The darkies were warping along merrily now, their skins glistening with their recent wetting. Behind, lay such a very hell of raging surf as to set me wondering whether we could really have come through it and lived.

"Blanked heavy bar on to-day, mister," said the skipper of the lighter, cramming a pipe from a rubber pouch. "My word, but you've got a ducking. Five bob please, for landing you."

I handed over the amount, and asked him about accommodation.

"Keightley's—up yonder," he said. "That's the only hotel on the West bank. There's a German shanty a mile or so higher up t'other bank, but you'll be better here. Going on to 'King,' I take it?"

"Where?"

"'King'—King Williamstown," he explained.

I was about to reply that I was a picked-up castaway, but thought better of it in time. Such would be presumed to be destitute, and thus might find initial difficulties as to accommodation. So I only answered that that would do me.

Now a most weird noise attracted my attention, and I found that it proceeded from a sight hardly less weird. Covering a ricketty jetty which we were slowly approaching, a crowd of strange beings were preparing for our reception after their own fashion. Some were clothed in brick red blankets and some were clothed in nothing, but all were smeared from head to foot with red ochre— and, as they swayed and contorted, a thunder of deep bass voices accompanying the high yelling recitative of him who led the chant, and beat time in measured stamping on the boards, I wondered that the structure did not collapse and strew the river with the lot of them. But their wild aspect and the grinning and contortions gave me the idea of a crowd of hugely exaggerated baboons in the last stage of drunken frenzy. But they were not drunk at all. It was only the raw savage, disporting himself after his own form of lightheadedness.

Up to this time my ideas as to the Kafir of South-Eastern Africa had been vague. If I had thought of him at all it had been as a meek, harmless kind of black, rather downtrodden than otherwise, and to whom a kick and a curse would constitute a far more frequent form of reward than a sixpence. But now as I stepped upon the jetty at East London, my views on that head underwent a complete and lasting change. For these ochre-smeared beings were brawny savages, at once powerful and lithe of frame and with a bold independent look in their rolling eyes, which, although their countenances were in the main good-humoured, seemed to show that they were able and willing to hold their own if called upon to do so. More than one of the group towered above me, and I am not short. They crowded around, vociferating in their own tongue, and tried to seize the bundle I carried—this, by the way, contained a change of clothing which Morrissey had insisted on my accepting—and I began to think of showing fight, when the surf-boat skipper came to my aid with the explanation that they merely wanted to carry it for me, for a consideration. But I was glad to get rid of the vociferous musky-smelling crowd—little thinking what strange and wild experiences awaited me yet at the hands of the savage inhabitants of this land, of whom these were fair representatives. And here I was, thrown up, as it were, upon this inhospitable coast, without a dry stitch of clothing upon me.

Soon I found myself the fortunate possessor of a small whitewashed room in the only "hotel" the place boasted—and its leading features were flies and various weird and unknown specimens of the beetle tribe, both small and great, which, attracted by the light, would come whizzing in, blundering against the greasy flare which had attracted them—to their discomfiture, or into my face—to mine; but at length I fell asleep, to the unintermittent thunder of the surf upon the bar. But the said sleep was troubled and fitful. The door, half glazed, was door and window combined, and the night being sultry, this must perforce be left open, and in the result I don't know how many frogs startled me out of my slumbers by a weird, searching croak right at my bedside, but I do know that at least three rats were playing hopscotch upon my counterpane at once. And these, and other unconsidered trifles, ensured that precious little sleep fell to my lot the first night I passed upon the soil of Southern Africa, whither I had been thrown under so strange and unforeseen a combination of circumstances.

Chapter Five.

Of an Early Adventure.

I awoke in the morning feeling but poorly rested, and having assimilated an indifferent breakfast, which however was quite passable after four weeks of ship fare, set out to interview the manager of the local branch of the Standard Bank. I was business man enough to feel misgivings as to any success attending the object of my interview, and so far was justified by results. The manager—a youngish man, and the usual Scotchman—listened to my story politely enough—sympathetically too. But when it came to hard business, opening an account pending the time I could communicate with my own bankers, the difficulty began. He did not exactly disbelieve my story: my proposal to bring forward Captain Morrissey in corroboration went far against that. But then how could Captain Morrissey vouch as to my means? On my own showing he could by no possibility do so, and indeed to no one, in view of my business experience as aforesaid, did such an argument more fully appeal than to myself. As to reference home, why, England in those days was over three weeks distant, otherwise seven or eight before an answer could be had. Didn't I know any one locally who could vouch for me? Of course I didn't—considering the circumstances under which I had found myself here. Well, he was exceedingly sorry he could not accommodate me—on his own responsibility. He would, however, refer the matter to the general manager, and would then be only too happy, etc., etc. And so I was very politely bowed out.

Well, I couldn't blame him. Business is business, and I might have been just the predatory adventurer he had no proof I was not. But for all that I went out feeling very disconsolate. My seven pounds nine and a halfpenny wouldn't last long, and I had already begun to bore into it. What was I to do next—yes—what the devil was I to do next?

I thought I would cross the river for one thing, and take a walk along the shore on the other side. I believe I had a sort of foolish idea that the mere sight of the *Kittiwake* lying close in at anchor, constituted a kind of link between other times and my homeless and friendless condition on this strange and far away shore; and some thoughts of shipping on board her as an able seaman, and so working my passage round home, even entered my head. Anyway, I crossed over on the pontoon, and walking along the bush road which skirted the east bank, at length came out upon the green slope which stretches down to the sandy beach within the bight of the roadstead.

The vessels were riding to their anchorage, and the rattle of swinging out cargo, and the yells and chatter of Kafirs working the surf boats, was borne across the water. The bar had gone down considerably since the previous day, yet there was still some surf on, and it came thundering up the beach, all milky and blue in the radiance of the unclouded sun—which said sun began to wax uncommonly warm, by the same token. However, the voyage had inured me to tropical heat, which this wasn't; wherefore I sat down to take a rest, and smoke a pipe.

Now as I sat there, moodily gazing out to seaward, an object caught my eye. It was beyond the further line of surf, and it looked uncommonly like the head of something swimming. Yet, who would be fool enough to swim out beyond that line of rollers, with their powerful and dangerous undertow? Besides, I had heard that sharks were plentiful on that coast.

I stared at the thing as it rose on the summit of a long wave. Yes, it was a head, and—great heaven! it was the head of a child; the sunlight falling full upon a little white face, and just a glimpse of gold as it touched the head, revealed that much beyond a doubt. And, as though to add to the mystery of the situation, a cry rang out over the roar of the breakers, which sounded most startlingly like a cry for help.

I was on my feet in a moment. Not a soul was in sight along the shore. In less than another moment I had thrown off my coat and kicked off my boots, and as I dashed into the surf another cry came pealing through the roar—this time more urgent, more piteous than before. I shouted in encouragement and then it required all my strength and experience in the water to get through that hell of boiling breakers, and avoid being rolled and pounded and thrown ignominiously back half drowned. Were it not indeed that I am a strong swimmer, and, what is better still, thoroughly at home in the water, such is precisely what would have happened.

A horrible fear came upon me as I got beyond the broken line. Was I too late? Then the object of my search rose upon the wave within a few yards of me.

It was, as I had thought, the face of a child—of a pretty little girl of twelve or thirteen. She wore a blue bathing dress, which allowed plenty of freedom for swimming, and her golden-brown hair was gathered in a thick plait. But in the large blue eyes was a look of terror, a kind of haunted look.

"Here, you're all right now," I shouted as I reached her. "Don't be scared. Lean on me, and rest. Then we'll swim in together. Hold on to my shoulder now. That's right."

The little one seemed exhausted, for she could hardly gasp out—

"We must go in quick. Sharks—two of them—after me," and again she stared wildly over her shoulder with that terrified and haunted look. And indeed a very uncomfortable feeling came over myself, for there I was, over a hundred yards from shore, treading water, with a badly frightened child hanging on to my shoulder, the breakers in front and this other peril behind.

Peril indeed! Seldom, if ever, have I known such a chilling of the blood as that which now went through my frame. A black glistening object was sliding through the water, five-and-twenty yards away, perhaps less—a rakish triangular object, with which I was familiar enough by that time to identify as the dorsal fin of a shark, and a large one too. And, great heaven! even nearer still on the other side was another of those dreadful glistening fins.

"We'll scare them effectually," I said, with a hollow and ghastly grin of assumed levity. And springing half out of the water I emitted a most fiendish yell, while falling back again with a mighty splash. It was effective, for the two hateful objects sheered off, gliding away a short distance—but only a short distance.

"Come now," I said, making a most prodigious splashing. "We must get in. Swim with me. Hold my hand if you are tired."

"No, I'm all right now," said the plucky little thing, beginning to strike out quite easily and naturally. Then I saw her face pale, and she stole a quick, terrified look over her shoulder, and I felt mine do ditto. For there—keeping pace with us, one on each side, and about the same distance at which we had first sighted them, moved the two horrors. They were trying to get ahead of us, to cut us off before we could reach the broken water, wherein they dare not venture.

I once knew a man who had escaped from the foundering of the ill-fated *Birkenhead*, and he attributed his exemption to the fact that time had lacked wherein to divest himself of his clothing before starting to swim ashore—for two sailors, who had been able to strip, were pulled under, one on each side of him. And now this idea flashed a wonderful hope into my mind, for I was almost fully clothed and my little companion wore a bathing dress. But her strokes were quick and spasmodic, and she panted. Terror was sapping her natural confidence in the water.

"This won't do," I cried in a loud hectoring voice. "Keep cool, can't you, and don't be a little idiot."

The bullying tone told, as I intended it should. The look she gave me was amusingly resentful and contemptuous. But she ceased to swim wildly. At the same time our slimy enemies increased their distance, doubtless alarmed at the sound of my voice, which I also intended. To my unspeakable and heartfelt relief we were now on the upheave of the curling combers, and those horrible fins were still behind.

But we were not out of the wood yet—no, not by any means; for here before us lay a peril almost as formidable in itself. My little companion swam gracefully and with ease, but when we came within the breakers I kept tight hold of her, and indeed such precaution was needed, for she began to regain her terrors as the huge combers whirled us high in the air, to throw us, half smothered into a hissing cauldron of milky foam. However, they threw us forward, and by using my judgment I managed so that we should ride more and more in on the crest of each roller. And the undertow at the very last proved the most difficult of all to withstand, and twice we were dragged irresistibly backward, to be pounded by the breaking thunder of the next onrushing comber. At last we were through, and I believe but for the incentive afforded by the very act of saving life, I should have collapsed—anyway, the child could never have gained that beach unaided.

We stood, panting and dripping, and looking at each other for some moments. Then I said, as I pulled on my boots—

"Well, young lady, you seem to have had something of a swim. Where did you go into the water, and what on earth made you venture out so far, may I ask?"

She explained that she was staying at a seaside camp whose tents were pitched just beyond a few rocks a little way further on. The water was sheltered there, and there was no difficulty in getting a smooth swim. But she had somehow got too far to the right, and just as she was turning to come in again, she had seen the triangular fin of a shark cleaving the surface at no great distance, and coming towards her—then another, much nearer. This, together with the knowledge of the distance necessary to return, unless she could try to land through the surf, had unnerved and flurried her, resulting in exhaustion.

"Well, I believe it's jolly lucky for you I happened to be at hand," I said reprovingly. "Now, don't you go running any such silly risks again, or you may not get off so easily. You'd better cut back now, and get dressed, or you'll catch cold."

"No fear. The sun's much too hot for that," she answered, laughing up into my face.

She was, as I have said, a pretty child, with large blue eyes and a clear skin somewhat sun-tanned. She had a pretty voice too, and spoke with a peculiar intonation, not unpleasing, and a little way of dipping the letter "r" where it occurred to end a word—which I afterwards found was the prevailing method of speech among most of those born in the Cape Colony.

I picked up my hat and coat intending to see her safely, at any rate until within sight of her people.

"What's your name?" I said, as we walked along, at first in silence.

"Iris."

"Iris—what?"

But before she could answer, two girls appeared round the pile of rocks, which we had nearly gained. They looked startled at seeing me, then scared, and no doubt I looked a little wild, for a rational white man walking along the beach in soaked and dripping clothes was not an everyday object. Then they advanced shyly and somewhat awkwardly, and it occurred to me that they did not look quite the equals in the social scale of my little friend.

The latter whispered to me, hurriedly and concernedly.

"Don't tell them anything about me—about finding me as you did. I shall never be allowed to go into the water again. Don't tell them. Promise you won't."

What could I do but give the required promise? Then the little one, with a hurried good-bye, skipped off to join the two, who were awaiting her—rather awkwardly—at a little distance off.

"Ungrateful little animal!" I thought to myself. "She would never have seen land again but for me—that's as certain as that she's on it now."

Child-like, her first thought had been for herself—smothering even the barest expression of thanks. I did not want to be thanked for saving her little life, still I thought she might have shown a trifle more appreciation, child though she was. And as I wended my way back, my clothes fast drying on me under the powerful rays of the midday sun, another and a meaner thought struck me, begotten, I hope, of my lonely and forlorn condition. I did not want gratitude; still, the incident might have availed to make me friends of some sort in this strange and far away land, and of such I had none.

In a state of corresponding depression, I sat down to dinner. There were two other men present, rough specimens of the small agricultural class, who performed marvellous feats of attempted knife swallowing; and as I divided my energies between keeping off the swarming flies and taking in the necessary sustenance, I began to wonder what on earth I should do to get a living until the two months necessary to hear from England had elapsed. Indeed, I began almost to regret my steady refusal of Captain Morrissey's proffered loan; for that prince of good fellows had been really hurt because I had refused to borrow a ten pound note from him—which, he said, was most of what he had with him; but what did he want with money anyhow then, he urged, being on board ship all the time?

"Say, mister!" said a voice in my ear, accompanied by a characteristically familiar touch on the shoulder. "There's a gentleman asking for you."

I looked up and beheld the frowzy, perspiring barkeeper, in his usual shirt-sleeves. A visitor for me? Why, Morrissey, of course—or was it the bank manager come to say he had thought better of his refusal, and I could open an account within modest limits right there? The grimy barkeeper seemed as an angel with a message as I followed him somewhat hastily to the front room. Then disappointment awaited. The room contained neither of these, but one stranger, and him I didn't know from Adam.

Chapter Six.

Of the Unexpected.

The stranger, who was looking out of the window, turned as I entered, and I saw a tall good-looking young fellow, some three or four years my junior.

"Don't you know me?" he said, with a smile.

"I'm afraid I don't," I answered, feeling thoroughly puzzled, and the thought flashed through my mind he must be some relative of the child I had rescued.

"I wondered if you would," he went on. "I'm Matterson—Brian Matterson. We were at old Wankley's together."

"By Jove! Why, so it is. I'm awfully glad to meet you. It's small wonder if I didn't know you again, Matterson. You were a youngster then, and it must be quite a dozen years ago, if not more."

"About that," he answered; and by this time we were "pump-handling" away like anything.

"How on earth did you find me out, though?" I asked. "I don't know a soul in the land."

"That's just it. I got on your spoor by the merest fluke. Was in at the bank this morning on business, and while I was yarning with Marshbanks I saw your card lying on the table. That made me skip, I can tell you, for I thought there couldn't be two *Kenrick* Holts; if it had been Tom or George, or any name like that, of course it wouldn't have been so certain. Marshbanks said you had called on him not very long before me, and he was sorry to have to disappoint you, because you looked a decent sort of chap; but still, biz was biz."

"Oh, I don't blame him in the least," I said. "I fully recognise that maxim myself."

"Well, I told him if you were the chap I thought, he need raise no further *indaba* about accommodating you, because I'd take the responsibility. So we'll stroll round presently and look him up, and put the thing all right."

"Awfully good of you, Matterson. In fact, you've no idea what running against you like this means to me, apart from the ordinary pleasure of meeting an old pal. Did the manager tell you how I got here?"

"Yes, and it struck me that a shipwrecked mariner leaving home suddenly like you did might have come, well—hum!—rather unprepared, so I lost no time in putting you right with Marshbanks. And now, what are your plans?"

"Why, to get back home again."

"I wouldn't hurry about that if I were you. Why not come and stay with us a bit? The governor'll be delighted, if you can put up with things a bit plain. We can show you a little of the country, and what life on a stock farm is like. A little in the way of sport too, though there's a sight too many Kafirs round us for that to be as good as it ought."

"My dear chap, I shall be only too delighted. You can imagine how gay and festive I've been feeling, thrown up here like a stranded log, not knowing a living soul, and with seven pound nine and a halfpenny—and that already dipped into—for worldly wealth until I could hear from home."

"By Jove! Is that all? Well, it's a good job I spotted your card on Marshbanks' table."

"Here, we'll have a drink to our merry meeting," I said, rapping on the table by way of hailing the perspiring barman aforesaid. "What's yours, Matterson?"

"Oh, a French and soda goes down as well as anything. Only, as this is my country, the drinks are mine too, Holt. So don't put your hand in your pocket now. Here's luck! Welcome to South Africa."

We had been schoolfellows together, as Brian Matterson had said, but the three or four years between our ages, though nothing now, had been everything then. I remembered him a quiet, rather melancholy sort of boy on his first arrival from his distant colonial home, and in his capacity of new boy had once or twice protected him from the rougher pranks of bigger fellows. But he had soon learned to take his own part, never having been any sort of a fool, and, possibly by reason of his earliest training, had turned out as good at games and athletics as many bigger and older fellows than himself. We had little enough to do with each other then by reason of the difference in our ages, yet we might have been the greatest chums if the genuine cordiality wherewith he now welcomed me here—in this, to me, distant and strange country—went for anything.

We strolled round to the bank, and the manager was full of apologies, but I wouldn't hear any, telling him I quite understood his position, and would almost certainly have acted in the same way myself. Then, our business satisfactorily disposed of, Brian and I went round to a store or two to procure a little clothing and a trunk, for my wardrobe was somewhat scanty. But such things as I could procure would not have furnished good advertisements for a first-rate London tailor or hosier.

"Don't you bother about that, Holt," Brian said. "You don't want much in the way of clothes in our life. Fit doesn't matter—wear and comfort's everything." And I judged I could not do better than be guided by his experience.

We were to start early the next morning, and had nearly two days' drive before us. This was not their district town, Brian explained to me; indeed, it was the merest chance that he was down here at all, but his father and a neighbour or two had been trying the experiment of shipping their wool direct to England, and he had come down to attend to it. He was sending the waggons back almost empty, but we would return in his buggy. At my suggestion that my surprise visit might prove inconvenient to his people he simply laughed.

"We don't bother about set invites in this country, Holt," he said. "Our friends are always welcome, though of course they mustn't expect the luxury of a first-class English hotel. You won't put us out, so make your mind quite easy as to that."

Late in the afternoon we parted. Brian was due to drive out to a farm eight or ten miles off—on business of a stock-dealing nature—and sleep, but it was arranged he should call for me in the morning any time after sunrise.

There is a superstition current to the effect that when things are at their worst they mend, and assuredly this last experience of mine was a case confirming it. An hour or so ago here was I, stranded, a waif and a stray, upon a very distant shore, a stranger in a strange land, wondering what on earth I was going to do next, either to keep myself while in it or get out of it again. And now I had all unexpectedly found a friend, and was about to set forth with that friend upon a pleasure visit fraught with every delightful kind of novelty. There was one crumple in the rose-leaf, however. We were starting early the next morning, and I should have no opportunity of seeing Morrissey and my excellent friends of the *Kittiwake* again. I went round to the agents, however, and inquired if there was no way of sending any note or message to the ship, and was disgusted to find that there was none that day. The bar had risen again in the afternoon, and there was no prospect of any one from the shipping in the roadstead coming ashore. So I left a note for the captain, expressing—well, a great deal more than I could ever have told in so many words.

I was up in good time next morning, and had just got outside of a muddy concoction whose principal flavour was wood-fire smoke, and was euphemistically termed coffee, when Brian Matterson drove up in a Cape cart.

"Hallo, Holt," he sang out. "You're in training early. You see, with us a fellow has to turn out early, if only that everybody else does, even if he himself has nothing particular to do. Well, in this case I might have given you a little longer, because I've got to pick up a thing or two at the store, and it won't be open just yet, and then my little sister's coming to have a look at me at the pontoon by way of good-bye. She's staying with some people down here at a seaside camp—I brought her down when I came four days ago—and wants to say good-bye, you know. She's a dear little kid, and I wouldn't disappoint her for anything. Now trot out your luggage, and we'll splice it on behind."

We got hold of a sable myrmidon who was "boots" and general handyman about the place, a queer good-humoured aboriginal with his wool grown long and standing out like unravelled rope around his head, and having hauled out my new trunk, bound it on behind the trap with the regulation raw hide *reim*. Then we thought we might as well have some breakfast before starting, and did.

It was about seven o'clock when we started, but the sun's rays were already manifest, even through the shelter of the canvas awning. The horses, a pair of flea-bitten roans, were not much to look at, being smallish, though sturdy and compact, but in hard condition, and up to any amount of work. We picked up some things at the store, and then it seemed to me we had hardly started before we pulled up again. There was the white of a sunshade by the roadside, and under it the flutter of a feminine dress. I recognised one of the girls who had come out to meet the little one to whose aid I had so opportunely come the day before, and—great heavens!—with her was my little friend herself.

"Hallo, Iris," sung out Brian Matterson. "Get up, now; I've got to take you back. Just had a note from Beryl to say you re to go back at once. Jump up, now."

The little one laughed, showing a row of white teeth, and shook her pretty head.

"No fear," she replied. "Keep that yarn for next time, Brian." Then, catching sight of me, she started and stared, reduced to silence. The while I was conscious of being introduced to Miss Somebody or other, whose name I couldn't for the life of me catch, and, judging from the stiff awkwardness wherewith she acknowledged the introduction, I was sure she could not catch mine. Then, in answer to some vehement signalling on the part of the child, Brian got down and went a little way with her apart, where the two seemed immersed in animated conversation, leaving me to inform the awkward girl that it was a fine morning and likely to continue hot, and to indulge in similar banalities.

Brian reascended to his seat, and relieved me of the reins. I, the while, faithful to my plighted word, showed no sign of ever having seen the child before, seeming indeed to see a certain reminder of the same in her sparkling pretty little face as she half-shyly affected to make my acquaintance. Brian kissed her tenderly, and we drove on. But before we had had gone far he turned on me suddenly.

"Holt, I don't know how to thank you, or what to say. I've just heard from Iris what you did yesterday. Man, you saved her life—her *life*, do you hear?—and what that means to me—to us—why, blazes take it, you've seen her!—I don't know how I can convey the idea better."

He was all afire with agitation—indeed, to such an extent as to astonish me, for I had set him down as rather a cool customer, and not easily perturbed. Now he continued to wax eloquent, and it made me uncomfortable. So I endeavoured to cut him short.

"All right, old chap. It isn't worth jawing about. Only too glad I was on hand at the time. Besides, nothing at all to a fellow who can swim. I say, though, I was admiring the way the little girl was at home in the water; still, she's small, and those beastly breakers have a devil of an undertow, you know. She oughtn't to be allowed out like that with nobody to look after her."

"That's just it. But she bound me to secrecy, like she did you, for fear of not being allowed in again. I made her promise not to do it again though, as a condition of keeping dark."

And then he went on to expatiate on Miss Iris' swimming perfections, and indeed every other perfection, to an extent that rather prejudiced me against her if anything, as likely to prove a spoilt handful. However, it got him out of the gratitude groove, which was all I wanted just then.

That couple of days' journey was quite one of the most delightful experiences of my life. Our way lay over beautiful rolling country dotted with flowering mimosa, and here and there intersected with a dark forest-filled kloof; and bright-winged birds flashed sheeny from our path, and on every hand the hum of busy insects made music on the warm air. Yes, it was warm; in the middle of the day very much so. But the evening was simply divine, in its hushed dewiness rich with the unfolding fragrance of innumerable subtle herbs, for we took advantage of a glorious moon to travel in the coolness. Now and again we would pass a large Kafir kraal, whose clustering beehive-shaped huts stood white in the moonlight, and thence an uproar of stamping and shouting, accompanying the rhythm of a savage song, showed that its wild denizens were holding high festivity at any rate; and the sound of the barbarous revel rising loud and clear upon the still night air, came to me with an effect that was wholly weird and imposing.

"Seems as if I had suddenly leaped outside civilisation altogether," I remarked as we passed one of these kraals, whose inhabitants paused in their revelry to send after us a long loud halloo, partly good-humoured, partly insolent. And I gave my companion the benefit of my preconceived notions of the Kafir, whereat he laughed greatly.

"It's funny how these notions get about, Holt," he said. "Now you have seen a glimpse of your meek, down-trodden black—only he's generally red—since you landed, and you can the more easily realise it when I tell you he'd cut all our throats with the greatest pleasure in life if he dared. There are enough of them to do it any night in the year; but, providentially, there's never any cohesion among savages, and these chaps won't trust each other, which is our salvation, for they simply swarm as to numbers. What do you say? Shall we outspan and make a night of it on the veldt? There's an accommodation house a mile or so further on, but it's a beastly hole, and the people none too civil."

Of course I voted for camping, and as Brian's forethought had provided a supply of cold meat and bread and cheese, as well as a bottle of grog, we fared (relatively) sumptuously, and thereafter the last thing I knew was my first pipe dropping out of my mouth very soon indeed after I had lighted it.

We inspanned early the next morning, and as we progressed our way became more hilly. Thick bush came down to the road in many places, and twice we forded a drift of a river, whose muddy and turbid current rose to the axles. The high broken country, copiously bush-clad, was delightful to the eye, but oh, the heat of the sun in those scorching valley bottoms, where, when we were not jolting over uneven masses of stone, were wallowing painfully through inches and inches of thick red dust. Now and then we would pass a string of transport waggons, or a traveller on horseback, and in the middle of the day we outspanned at a farm of the rougher kind. Towards evening we entered a long, wild, beautiful valley resonant with the cooing of doves and other sounds of evening peace, the bleating of homing flocks and the lowing of cattle; and as we rounded a bush-clad spur and a homestead came into view I felt no surprise that Brian Matterson should turn to me with the remark—

"Here we are at last, Holt; and there's Beryl, on the look-out for us."

Chapter Seven.

Beryl.

He reined up the Cape cart at the gate of a picturesque verandah-fronted house which stood against a background of wild and romantic bush scenery. Not for this, however, had I any eyes at that moment; only for the personality which was framed as it were within a profusion of white cactus blossoms which overhung the garden gate.

"Well, Beryl!" he sang out, as we got out of the trap. "Here's an old school chum I picked up by the merest fluke down at East London. I brought him out here to see a little African life, so for the present I'll hand him over to you. Give him a cool chair on the stoep, and a ditto drink, while I go and see to the outspanning, and to things in general. Dad still away, I suppose?"

"Yes. He'll be back this evening, though. I'm expecting him every minute."

"So long, then."

Now I have already explained that I am by nature a reticent animal, and may add that I have a sneaking horror of being taken for a susceptible one. Wherefore I had refrained from questioning Brian on the way hither, as to the outward appearance or inner characteristics of his elder sister, and he, while mentioning the fact that he had another sister, who kept house for them—for their mother was long since dead—and a younger brother, had not entered into details.

But it would be idle to pretend I had not been indulging, and that mightily, in all sorts of speculation upon the subject, and that within my own mind. Would she resemble the little one to whose aid I had come—prove a grown-up replica of her? If so, she would be something to look at, I concluded. Yet, now that I beheld her, my first impression of Beryl Matterson was a strange mingling of interest and disappointment. Tall and very graceful of carriage, she stood there, with outstretched hand of welcome. The tint of the smooth skin was that of a dark woman, yet she had eyes of a rich violet blue—large, deep, thoughtful—and her abundant brown hair was drawn back in a wavy ripple from the temples.

But that her glance, so straight and scrutinising as it met mine, became melting and tender as it rested upon her brother, I should have set her down as of a cold disposition, and withal a trifle too resolute for a woman, especially for one of her age. As it was, I hardly knew what to think. She did not greatly resemble Brian, who though also tall and handsome was very dark; yet I suspected his to be the gentler disposition of the two.

"You are very welcome, Mr Holt," she said. "How strange that Brian should have met you down there."

"It was not only strange but providential, for I was literally a shipwrecked mariner thrown up on your shore without a dry stitch on me."

And I told her briefly the plight I had found myself in, when Brian had come to the rescue. She listened with great interest.

"Well, I am more than ever glad he did. But what an experience! The landing one, though, I have been through myself; the bar at East London can be too terrific for words. By the way, we have a little sister staying down there now with some friends. We thought the sea-bathing would do her good, and she's so fond of it. Did you see her, perhaps?"

"Yes. She met us outside the town to say good-bye. What a pretty child she is."

"She is, and nicely she gets spoiled on the strength of it," laughed Beryl, but the laugh was wholly a pleasant one, without a tinge of envy or resentment in it.

We chatted a little, and then she proposed we should stroll out and look at the garden and some tiny ostrich chicks she was trying to rear, and flinging on a large rough straw hat which was infinitely becoming, she led the way, down through an avenue of fig trees, and opened a light gate in the high quince hedge.

Then as I stood within the coolness of the garden, which covered some acreage of the side of the slope, I gained a most wonderful impression of the place that was destined to prove my home for a long time to come, and in whose joys and sorrows—yes, and impending tragedies of dark vendetta and bloodshed—I was fated to be associated. Below the house lay the sheep kraals, and already a woolly cataract was streaming into one of the thorn-protected enclosures, while another awaited its turn at a little distance off. The cattle kraal, too, was alive with dappled hides, and one unintermittent "moo" of restless and hungry calves, while a blue curling smoke reek from the huts of the Kafir farm servants rose upon the still evening atmosphere. What is there about that marvellous African sunset glow? I have seen it many a time since, under far different conditions—under the steamy heat of the lower Zambesi region, and amid piercing cold with many degrees of frost on the high Karoo; in the light dry air of the Kalahari, and in the languorous, semi-tropical richness of beautiful Natal; but never quite as I saw it that evening, standing beside Beryl Matterson. It was as a scene cut out of Eden, that wondrous changing glow which rested upon the whole valley, playing upon the rolling sea of foliage like the sweep of golden waves, striking the iron face of a noble cliff with a glint of bronze, then dying, to leave a pearly atmosphere redolent of distilling aromatic herbs, tuneful with the cooing of myriad doves and the whistle of plover and the hum of strange winged insects coming forth on their nightly quests.

"Let's see. How long is it since you and Brian saw each other last, Mr Holt?" said my companion as we strolled between high quince hedges.

"Why, it must have been quite twelve years, rather over than under. And most of the time has not been good, as far as I was concerned. The financial crash that forced me to leave school when I did, kept me for years in a state of sedentary drudgery for a pittance. Something was saved out of the wreck at last, but by that time I had grown 'groovy' and fought shy of launching out into anything that involved risk. I preferred to keep my poor little one talent in a napkin, to the possibility of losing it in the process of turning it into two."

She looked interested as she listened. The face which I had thought hard grew soft, sympathetic, and wholly alluring.

"There's a good deal in that," she laughed. "I must say I have often thought the poor one-talent man was rather hardly used. By the way, when Brian was sent to England to school it was with the idea of making a lawyer or a doctor of him, but he would come back to the farm. It was rather a sore point with our father for quite a long time after, but now he recognises that it is all for the best. My father is not what the insurance people call a 'good' life, Mr Holt."

"I'm very sorry to hear that. What is wrong? Heart?"

"Yes. But I am boring you with all these family details, but having been Brian's school chum seems to make you almost as one of ourselves."

"Pray rid yourself of the impression that you are boring me, Miss Matterson—on the contrary, I am flattered. But I must not obtain your good opinion under false pretences. The fact is, Brian and I were not exactly school chums. There was too much difference between our ages—at that time, of course; which makes it all the more friendly and kind of him to have brought me here now."

"Oh, that doesn't make any difference. If you weren't chums then you will be now, so it's all the same."

Then we talked about other things, and to my inquiries relating to this new land—new to me, that is—Beryl gave ready reply.

"You will have to return the favour, Mr Holt," she said with a smile. "There are many things I shall ask you about by-and-by. After all, this sort of life is a good deal outside the world, and I have never been to England, you know. I am only a raw Colonial."

I forget what answer I made; probably it was an idiotic one. But the idea of associating "rawness" with this well-bred, self-possessed, attractive girl at my side, seemed so outrageous that in all probability I overdid the thing in striving to demonstrate its absurdity.

On regaining the house we found Brian, who had just returned from counting in the flocks. He was not alone. Two Kafirs—tall, finely-built savages, their blankets and persons coloured terra-cotta red with ochre—stood at the steps of the stoep conversing with him, the mellow bass of their sonorous language and their far from ungraceful appearance and attitude lending another picturesque element to the rich unfamiliarity of the surroundings. They, however, were just taking their leave, bestowing upon us a quick, inquisitive glance, and a farewell salutation as they turned away.

"Two more of Kuliso's wandering lambs, Beryl," said Brian, with a significant laugh, as we joined him. "Yet none of ours, or sheep either, have vanished this time, so I suppose we ought to consider ourselves fortunate. The count is correct. By the way, Holt, I'm afraid one of the vicissitudes common to this country has deferred supper for a little. We can't do better than sit out here, so long."

There were cosy cane chairs upon the stoep, and as we sat chatting I said—

"Who is Kuliso?"

Brian laughed.

"One of the chiefs of the Ndhlambe location just east of us. A bad egg personally, and his clan is made up of 'prize' thieves and stock-lifters."

"But you, Miss Matterson," I went on. "Is it safe for you to go about alone among such neighbours?"

A glance of understanding, humorous withal, passed between brother and sister.

"Beryl is just about a dead shot, Holt," said the former quietly.

"But even then, what can one do against a number, and that one a—"

"A woman, you were going to say, Mr Holt," supplied that equable, resolute voice, that had already begun to charm me.

"Ha, ha!" laughed Brian. "Are you afraid to throw up your hat in the air, Holt, now, just as we sit? But never mind. It wouldn't be fair to spoil that new 'smasher' of yours. Mine's a very old one. Look now."

While he had spoken Beryl had disappeared within the house for a moment. Now she stood there holding a revolver—no toy, mind, but a real effective and business-like six-shooter. Up went Brian's hat, whirling in mid-air. Just as it rested stationary for a fraction of a second at its highest flight, there was a sharp report; the hat gave a spasmodic jerk, like a live thing, and began to fall. But before it touched ground there was another report. Struck again, it gave a leap, and went skimming away to the ground in sidelong flight.

"Magnificent, by Jove!" broke from me. But that she had lowered the still smoking weapon, Beryl had not moved. Brian, however, had sprung from his seat to retrieve his hat.

"Call that nothing, Holt?" he cried, pointing out two clean bullet holes—one through the brim, the other through the crown. "Good thing it wasn't yours, eh?"

"Yes, indeed."

"Brian, it's too bad of you, to make me show off in that way," said Beryl. "I can't think why I did it. Now I must go and see to things inside, or you two poor hungry creatures will get nothing to eat to-night."

She disappeared, and as the playful, chiding tone, the merrily deprecatory glance remained in my mind, I realised a strange impression. It seemed that all in a moment she had thrown aside that outer crust of reserve which she had worn for my benefit, and underneath I descried the real Beryl Matterson. And into a very sweet and alluring personality did my mental gaze seem to penetrate.

"Bushbuck chops, Holt," said Brian, as we sat down to supper, in the snug, well-lighted dining-room, which in the comfort and refinement of its appointments bore token of the hand of a presiding genius—to wit, Beryl. "Rather out of season, buck, just now; still, we shoot one now and then, if only as a change from the eternal sheep. Try them. New kind of grub for you, eh?"

I did try them, and found them perfect, as indeed everything on the table was, and this was a farm on the average scale. I have since been at many a similar place run on a large scale where the appointments were slovenly in comparison. But then such did not own Beryl Matterson as a presiding goddess. Afterwards we adjourned to the stoep.

"Beryl will join us directly, Holt," said Brian, as we lit our pipes. "She has to see to things a bit first. Girls over here have to do that, you know. I can tell you we should come off badly if they didn't."

Later on, when I got to my room at the end of the stoep, and turned in between snowy sheets, I appreciated what some of the aforesaid "seeing to things" on Beryl's part involved.

"I expect the governor and George'll sleep at Trask's to-night, and turn up first thing in the morning," declared Brian as it waxed late. And Beryl, who had long since joined us, concurred.

It was wholly delightful as we sat there chatting, in the soft night air—the range of hills opposite silvered and beautiful in the moonlight, and ever and anon the strange cry of bird or beast floating through the stillness, or the wailing whistle of plover circling above—and to me the experience was as strange as it was delightful. A day or two ago, I had felt lonely and forlorn indeed—a stranger in a strange land. Yet now here I was, in the most congenial surroundings beneath a hospitable roof whose inmates looked upon me as one of themselves and had made me thoroughly at home accordingly. And the fact that one of the said inmates was an unusually attractive girl did not, you may be sure, under the circumstances tend to lessen the feeling of thorough and comfortable enjoyment to which the situation caused me to give myself up. At last Brian began to yawn.

"Holt, old chap, you must excuse me," he said. "We turn out early here and have to turn in tolerably ditto."

I professed myself quite in accord with the idea. The fact was I felt just a little tired myself.

"So? Well, then, we'll have a glass of grog and turn in."

If I have dwelt upon the incidents of that first evening, I suppose it is because upon such one's first and most vivid impressions are invariably based.

Chapter Eight.

A New Life.

I awoke from a sound sleep, or rather was awakened by a knocking at the door. Remembering my disclaimer of susceptibility, I hardly like to own the persistency wherewith my dreams were haunted by visions of my hostess. But now the sun was already up, and as I shouted "Come in," the opening door admitted a broad dazzling flash of his new-born radiance together with the form of a small Kafir girl bearing a cup of coffee. Sounds, too, of busy life came from outside.

A shave and a cool refreshing tub, and it did not take me long to get into my clothes. There was no one about the house, except a Kafir girl sweeping the stoep, but I heard voices in the direction of the kraals, and thither wending I came upon a great enclosure filled with cattle, and the hissing squirt of milk into zinc pails told what was going forward. As I climbed over the gate, the voices increased in volume, and expressed anger, not to say menace. Then a sight met my eyes, causing me to move forward a little quicker.

Brian Matterson was standing at the further end, and, confronting him, a huge Kafir. The latter was talking volubly in his own tongue, whose rolling bass seemed to convey a ferocity which even to my inexperienced ear was unmistakable. Moreover, he seemed to emphasise his arguments, whatever they, were, with a very suggestive grip upon a pair of hardwood sticks, which he held one in each hand. But Brian, who was totally unarmed, stood, one hand in his trousers pocket, talking quietly, and absolutely and entirely at his ease.

Suddenly the savage, an evil-looking, ochre-smeared ruffian, raised his voice to a roar of menace, and at the same time one of the sticks whirled through the air. But Brian merely stepped back a pace, and then what followed was beautiful to behold. His fists were playing like the drumsticks of a kettledrum, and down went his towering assailant into the dust of the cattle kraal—then springing up, down he went again. It was all done in a moment, before I could even reach the spot.

"That you, Holt?" said Brian, without, however, taking his eyes off his discomfited adversary, to whom he continued to address some further remarks in the tongue of the Amaxosa, and who, shuffling along the ground, rose to his feet some little way off and slunk away out of the enclosure, snarling out a deep-toned running fire of what sounded not in the least like benediction.

"What's the row?" I said.

"Oh, nothing much. Rum thing, though, it should have happened the very first glimpse you get of us. Still, it had to be. That fellow, Sibuko, was with us here once, but we turned him off. He came back this morning, and it's my belief he came back on purpose to have a row—and he's got his wish."

"Rather," I said, in hearty admiration for the masterly way in which my former schoolfellow had reduced to order a formidable and muscular barbarian, an encounter with whom I myself would far rather have avoided than welcomed. "You did that well, Brian. Yet I don't remember you as a superlative bruiser at old Wankley's."

"Nor am I now. After all, it's nothing. These chaps can't use their fists, you know."

"How about their sticks?"

"Yes, that comes in. A smart Kafir with a couple of kerries is often a large contract—quickness is the great thing with either. Still, it's unpleasant, and I don't care about it. But you'll hardly believe me when I tell you the necessity may not arise once in a year. Only, you can't be defied on your own place. I told that chap to clear, and he answered point-blank that he wouldn't. There was only one way of settling that difference of opinion, you see."

And he turned to give an order to one of his Kafirs, calm, equable, as if nothing had happened.

"Have a smoke," he went on, "or is it too early for you? Yes? Oh well, perhaps a fellow is better in moderation. Though I expect you'll soon tumble into all our ways." And he filled and lighted his pipe, while we chatted, but not for a moment did his attention slacken from what he was engaged upon, the superintending of the milking to wit.

It was a lovely cloudless morning, and there was something in the clear dry atmosphere that was exhilarating in the extreme. How would I take to this sort of life? I thought to myself. Already the old life seemed far away, and all behind. The charm of this new life—its freedom and glorious climate—were settling upon me; why should I not embark in it? I had the means, if I started carefully and modestly. I did not imagine for a moment there was a fortune in it, but neither was there in the branch of business in which my lines had hitherto been cast. And somehow, woven in with such meditations was already the image of Beryl Matterson; which was quite too absurd, remembering that twenty-four hours ago I had never seen her.

"Don't you ever carry a six-shooter, Matterson?" I said, my mind reverting to the little difference of opinion I had just seen so effectually settled.

"Very seldom. You see, we are not outside the law here, and if I shot a fellow I should almost certainly find myself in a nasty awkward mess."

"What—even in self-defence?"

"Even then. The English law is curiously wooden-headed on some points. The 'sacredness of human life' is one of them, especially with a judge or two we have here who will always go against a white man in favour of a Kafir; and if you were known to habitually carry arms it would go further against you still."

"But what about your sister?"

"That's different. There isn't a jury on the frontier would convict a woman for shooting a Kafir, because they know perfectly well that such a thing couldn't happen except in a case of the direst necessity. In fact, there are far too few women and girls who are able to take care of themselves, and they all ought to be."

"I should very much think so," I said, and the time was to come when these remarks were destined to recur to my mind with vivid clearness and weighty force.

"Hallo!" said Brian, "here's the governor coming back." And following his glance, I saw the white tent of a trap coming down the road from the opposite direction to that of our way the evening before. A minute or so more and it drew up opposite the kraals.

"Don't say anything about what you've just seen, Holt," he went on, as we made our way to the gate. "He doesn't like that sort of thing, but for all that it's sometimes inevitable."

Of course I gave him the required assurance, and as we reached the gate the buggy pulled up, and there got out a strongly-built man of about fifty-five. He had a quiet-looking but determined face, which reminded me more of Beryl than of Brian, and a thick, full, brown beard, somewhat streaked with grey, and as Brian speedily introduced us his welcome of me was all that could be desired in the way of frank cordiality.

"I hope you will be able to make some stay with us, Mr Holt," he said. "You have spent the night here, and, I take it, have seen what we have to offer you; but such as it is, you are very welcome."

So this was Brian's father! I confess he inspired in me more than a feeling of cordiality—for it was one of admiration. I knew men pretty well by that time, and was a bit of a cynic on the subject; but now I saw before me one whom I read as rather a unique specimen—a man who would say what he meant, and who would act as his judgment dictated, no matter what the whole world might think—a man whose word would be as his bond, even though it were to his own detriment; in short, in this frontier stock-farmer I saw a man who, no matter where he might be put down, or under what circumstances, would be a very tower of reliability: cool, intrepid, sound of judgment, come good, come ill. And in all my subsequent friendship with Septimus Matterson, I never had cause to swerve one hair's breadth from my first impression—save in one instance only.

Now as two Kafirs came up to stand at the horses' heads, somebody else jumped out of the buggy—a boy to wit, whom Mr Matterson promptly introduced as his youngest son. He was a boy of about fourteen, a good-looking boy, but with a roving mischievous look in his face; a boy, in short, to whom I did not take one bit. Equally readily I could see that he did not take to me.

"Just out from England, hey?" said this hopeful. "Man, but you'll find it different here."

Now this was hardly the form of address to be looked for from a youngster of his tender age to a man very considerably his senior; moreover, there was something patronising about it which prejudiced me against the speaker; in fact, I set him down at once as an unlicked cub. But of course I showed no sign of what I was thinking, and the work Brian had been superintending being at an end, we all went round to count the flocks—I don't mean I bore any part in that operation, not then—and adjourned to the house for breakfast.

Chapter Nine.

Mainly Venatorial.

Beryl looked wholly fresh and delightful as she welcomed us, and it was hard to believe she had been up nearly three hours "seeing to things," as Brian put it. There was a good deal of talk, of wholly local interest, with regard to the expeditions of both father and son, and the results thereof, but even it was by no means without interest to me, for, after all, it let me into so much of the inner life of these strange new surroundings. Presently the young hopeful, looking up from a large plateful of oatmeal porridge and milk, observed—

"I say, Brian, let's go down to Zwaart Kloof this morning and try for a bushbuck ram."

"Well, I don't know. Yes. Perhaps Mr Holt would like to try his luck. What do you say, Holt?"

I said I'd like nothing better, but for the trifling drawback that I had no gun—being only a shipwrecked mariner who had come away with nothing but the clothes he stood up in. But this was speedily over-ruled. There were plenty of guns in the house. No difficulty about that.

"Can you shoot, Mr Holt?" said the youngster, planting both elbows on the table, and eyeing me with rather disdainful incredulity.

"Well, yes, I can shoot," I said. "Moderately, that is."

"But you're out from England," went on the cub, as though that settled the matter.

"George, you little ass, shut up, and go and tell them to saddle up Bles and Punch for us," said Brian. "You can ride Jack."

A volume of expostulation in favour of some other steed having been silenced by Brian in quiet and peremptory fashion, the hopeful went out.

"I'm afraid you'll find George rather a spoilt boy, Mr Holt," said Beryl. "He and Iris seem to get their own way more than they ought. They are the little ones, you see."

Of course I rejoined that it was quite natural—reserving my own opinion. In the case of the little girl it was candid: in the other—well "boy" to me is apt to spell horror; but a spoilt boy, and just a boy of George Matterson's age, well—to fit him, my vocabulary has never yet been able to invent an adequate superlative.

"You'd better have a shot gun, Holt," said Brian, as we started. "I always use one in thick bush; it's all close shooting."

He handed me a double Number Twelve bore, of first-rate make and poise, and kept in first-rate order too, and some treble A cartridges.

"You won't use all those. You'll be lucky if you get two fair and square shots," he remarked.

"Good luck, Mr Holt," called out Beryl after us.

I began to feel nervous. I was only an ordinary shot, and of this form of sport was, of course, utterly without experience—and said as much.

"You only shoot tame pheasants in England, don't you, Mr Holt?" said George, in a tone that made me wish I could turn him into one of the fowl aforesaid. Could it really be that this impudent young pup was Beryl's brother—or Brian's too, for the matter of that?

We cantered down the valley, then struck up a lateral spur, and rounding it came upon a deep kloof running far up into the hillside—its side black with dense bush, the *boerboen* and plumed euphorbia, and half a dozen other varieties whose names I didn't know then.

"Here, Tiger, Ratels, get to heel!" cried Brian, apostrophising the rough-haired dogs which had followed, all excited, at our horses' heels. "George, take Mr Holt on to the opening above the little krantz. You know where to post him. If he doesn't get a shot there he won't get one anywhere. Then come back to me."

We made a bit of a circuit, and some twenty minutes later found ourselves in a little open space, surrounded on three sides by dense bush, while the fourth seemed to be the brink of a precipitous fall in the ground. Here I was carefully posted in the combined cover of an ant-heap and a small mimosa.

"That's where they always break cover," whispered George. "Man, but you mustn't make a sound. Don't move—don't cough, even. So long."

Left alone, my nerves were all athrill with excitement, and I believe my hand shook. A couple of spreuws perched upon an adjoining bush, melodiously whistling, then, become mysteriously aware of my presence, flashed off—a pair of green-blue streaks, their note changed to one of alarm. Would they scare the game and turn it back? I thought agonisingly. Heavens! what if I should shoot badly, and miss? What a fool I should look—and this was, in a way, my *début*!

The space the quarry would have to cross was about twenty yards. Could I stop it in that distance? No, I was sure I could not. I was feeling far too shaky, far too eager—a nervous condition invariably fatal, at any rate in my own case, to effective execution.

The silence settled down around me, broken only by the occasional note of a bird. Then I started. What was that? The yapping of a dog, then another, then a chorus of excited yelps; and as it drew rapidly nearer I realised that they were on the track of something.

Exactly from the direction George had indicated, it came—a quick bounding rush. A noble antelope leapt out into the open. Its pointed, slightly spiral horns and dilated eye, the almost black hide with the white belly stripe, seemed photographed in my brain as I pressed the trigger, and—missed. Like a streak of dark lightning it shot across the open, and my left barrel spoke, a fraction of a second before it disappeared over the declivity. But in that fraction of a second I had seen the convulsive start, the unmistakable squirm, and could have hurrahed aloud.

I remained still, however, slipping in a couple of fresh cartridges. Another might come out. But it did not; instead, the dogs appeared hot foot on the scent, and close behind them George.

"Hallo, Mr Holt. Where's the buck?" cried that youth, with a derisive grin. "Man, but we drove him right over you."

"And I've driven him right over there," pointing to the brow of the declivity.

"So it seems. Man! but you won't get such a chance again in a hurry."

"Well, Holt? No luck, eh?" said Brian, appearing on the scene.

"Well, it depends on whether you look at it from my point of view or the buck's," I said with designed coolness. "If the latter, you're right."

"Eh? Why—"

Something of a clamour beneath interrupted him: the fierce worrying of dogs, and the half bellow, half scream, of a bush-buck ram in the last fight for his life. We did not pause a moment then. Flinging themselves from their horses—mine had been left much higher up—they plunged down, I following, leaping from rock to rock. There lay my quarry, unable to rise save on his forelegs, yet savagely menacing with his pointed horns the three dogs which were leaping and snarling frantically around him.

"He's done for—hit rather far back, though," said Brian, calling off the dogs. "Put another shot into him, Holt—forward this time."

I did, and the animal at once stiffened out, lifeless.

"*Maagtig!* but he's a fine ram," cried George, while congenially amusing himself by cutting the beast's throat. "You didn't hit him by accident, Mr Holt, hey?"

"Bad accident for the buck, anyway," said Brian with a dry laugh. "Well done, Holt. I congratulate you. Thirteen-inch horns! We'll have them done up for you as a trophy of your first bushbuck."

I was secretly not a little pleased with myself, as the buck, having been cleaned, was loaded up behind my saddle, and we took our way homewards, for Brian declared that we might be all day and not get anything like so good a chance again, without beaters and with only three dogs. Moreover, it was rather out of season, and they had come out solely on my account. I, however, was amply content; indeed, I sneakingly thought it just as well not to spoil the effect of my first prowess by potential and subsequent misses.

Yes, I felt decidedly satisfied with myself and at peace with all the world, as we drew near the homestead an hour or so later, with my quarry strapped behind my saddle. I heeded not—was rather proud, in fact—of the widening patch of gore which the movement of the horse caused to gather upon my trouser leg during our progress. The "fellow just out from home," the "raw Britisher," had vindicated himself. Even that young rascal George seemed to treat me with a shade of newly-fledged respect, and the very intonations in the voices of a couple of Kaffirs hanging around, as we rode up, were intelligible to me as witnessing to my prowess. Beryl and her father, who were sitting on the stoep when we arrived, came out to meet us.

"Well done, Mr Holt!" said the former. "I'm so glad you've had some luck."

"I think it was due to your last aspiration, Miss Matterson," I answered, feeling with a satisfaction wholly uncalled for by the occasion that somehow or other I had gone up in her estimation.

"Got him just above the krantz in the Zwaart Kloof, did you?" commented her father. "That's the place where you'll nearly always get a chance. I suppose this is your first experience of this kind of sport; but I can tell you there's many a man, not a bad shot either, who doesn't fall into it just so soon. George, take the horses round—let's see, keep Bles up though, I may want him later. And now we'll go in to dinner."

Throughout that welcome repast I was plying my host eagerly with questions as to the conditions of colonial life, and the vagaries of stock-farming in general; and wondering what a long while ago it seemed since I started for that fateful row at Whiddlecombe Regis, an unconscious voyage of discovery which should terminate in this.

"There are a sight too many Kafirs near us," he said, in answer to one of my questions. "That's the great drawback. They take too much toll of our stock, and besides, they have been getting restless lately. Some people set up a periodical scare, but I don't believe in that sort of thing. As they are here we must rub along with them as best we can, and I must say they bother me less than they do—or seem to do—some others. But you never know what to expect with savages."

"I suppose not," I answered, thinking of the tussle I had witnessed that morning, and remembering the malignant and vengeful looks of the defeated barbarian as he slunk out by the cattle kraal. "But couldn't they render the position—well, rather impossible for you, here, for instance, if they were to combine."

"That's just it—they can't combine. But if you know how to take them, and not expect to find angels under a red blanket and a daub of *root klip*, you can pull with them as well as with anybody else. Only you must never for a moment let them imagine you're afraid of them."

I little thought then how near was the time when I should witness Septimus Matterson's theory tested—and that severely. Yet that was to come, and it was only the beginning of a series of stirring events calling for readiness of resource and cool judgment and iron courage. The sun was shining now, the sky unclouded. Yet was the storm behind, gathering afar.

Chapter Ten.

Two Pacts.

It will be remembered that my first impressions as regarded Beryl Matterson savoured somewhat of disappointment. By the time I had dwelt a week beneath the same roof I could only marvel how such could have been the case. Now I had dwelt beneath it a month, and the prospect of life apart from her presence seemed not worth contemplating. To such a pass had things come.

What a time that had been—golden, idyllic! When I was not accompanying Brian or his father upon their rides or walks, on stock supervision or sport intent, I would inveigle Beryl forth on the plea of being put *au courant* with the flora and fauna of the country. Nor was the plea a fictitious one, for I had always had a leaning towards natural history, albeit precious little time or opportunity for indulging the same; but now, with such a companion, and such a taste in common! Ah, those long rides, the glorious sense of freedom and glowing enjoyment, the exhilaration of the atmosphere, the deep unclouded blue of the heavens, the rolling bush country—earth, air, foliage, all athrill with pulsating life, animal or insect life, never silent, never for a moment still—small wonder that those days should go by as in a very dream of Paradise!

But real life is not idyllic, only its episodes, and they but rarely; wherefore, fearing to outstay my welcome, I mooted the subject of moving on. Brian's blank stare of amazement was something to behold.

"Why, Holt, you've only just begun to know us," he said, "and it would be affectation to suppose you are not enjoying your stay, because any one could see that you are, even if you hadn't said so yourself. You can't leave us yet. You mustn't think of it—must he, dad?"

"Certainly not," declared Septimus Matterson with all his wonted decision. "Why, Iris would cry her eyes out. She's quite fallen in love with you, Holt."

For the little girl had returned home, and her seaside adventure—with me in the rôle of rescuing hero—had been made known. She had bound Brian to secrecy on the subject during her absence, lest her amusements should be restricted and herself placed under an irksome surveillance. Further than that he refused to be bound, nor did she herself desire it. On receipt of which tidings I really have the most confused recollection of what was said to me by each and all, or of the banalities I stuttered out as the nearest approach to a "suitable reply." The only definite thing that lives in my memory is the physical agony I strove to repress what time Septimus Matterson's iron grip enclosed my own far from delicate paw, while he declared that his house was henceforth as much my home as it was that of his own children, whenever and as long as I chose to make use of it—a declaration which went far to neutralise the excruciating experience which emphasised it, remembering that the said home was that of Beryl also. Even George was graciously pleased to approve of me, and in the result ceased to play me monkey tricks or to make me the butt of his covert impertinence.

"Man, Mr Holt, but that was fine!" he pronounced in reference to the episode. "*Ja*, I'd like to have been there! But I thought fellows from England couldn't do anything of that sort."

"Let it be a lesson to you then, George," I said with dignity, "that 'fellows from England' are not necessarily asses."

Then I felt foolish, for the remark savoured of a touch of complacent brag, and Beryl was a witness. But she seemed to read my inner confusion, and smiled reassuringly.

"There was Trask," went on the imp; "when he first came out he couldn't hit a house unless he was shut up inside it. He couldn't sit a horse either. *Ja*, we used to have fun out of Trask."

"I should say *Mr* Trask, George," said Beryl.

The correction was received with a lordly contempt, as the young rascal went on—

"Can you sit a bucking horse, Mr Holt?"

"Did you ever hear what the man said when he was asked if he could open oysters, George?" I said.

"No. What?"

"I've never tried."

He looked puzzled, then annoyed. Beryl and Iris broke into a peal of laughter.

"Don't see where any joke comes in," he grunted. "But why not have a try now, Mr Holt? There's Bontebok up in the stable. He always bucks when you first get on him. I'll go and tell Sixpence to saddle him up just now."

"You'll do nothing of the sort, George," pronounced Iris decisively. "You're a great deal too cheeky. I wonder Mr Holt stands it. Besides, we want him to go out with us."

That dear little girl! I was fond of her already, but more than ever now that she had come to my rescue in that whole-hearted and tactful fashion. For I did not want to make an exhibition of myself and furnish forth a circus entertainment with Beryl for audience; and it would have been difficult, unaided, to have backed out of what was in effect a challenge, without jeopardising my reputation.

"Another time, George. Another time," I answered loftily.

"Right you are; I'll tell them to keep Bontebok up," came the ready response. "He'll be livelier in the morning."

The young villain, you see, was not going to let me down so easily.

"But I may not be. Those circus tricks are all very well for an unfledged young monkey like you, George, but a middle-aged buffer isn't always on for that sort of game."

"Middle-aged buffer! That's good," jeered the young rascal. "Why, you and Brian were at school together."

"Oh, George, will you scoot?" interrupted Iris, emphasising the injunction with a far from gentle push. "You're getting such a bore, you know. Go and make yourself useful in some way, if you can. Get the air-gun and go and shoot some mouse birds. Brian and dad both want some tails to clean their pipes with."

"Can't. Dad'd object. It's Sunday."

"Well, anyhow—scoot. I don't want you. So long."

"I'm on for a swim in the dam," was the answer. "I'll go and rout out Brian."

Iris, you see, ruled the house, including George. Including me, I might add; but for me her rule was light. She was almost more grateful to me for keeping my own counsel upon it than for getting her out of her perilous predicament. Anyhow, we were great friends, and she teased me with the same freedom and whole-heartedness that she teased Brian, who idolised her; but in her bright, pretty, engaging little ways there was none of the covert impudence that characterised Master George's attempts at banter.

"I hear you are going to stay with us altogether, Mr Holt," she broke out suddenly an hour later as we were resting, having gained the objective of our Sunday afternoon stroll—a beautiful spot deep down in a kloof, where a pile of rocks all festooned with maidenhair fern overhung a large water-hole, and on the lower side steep upsweeping slopes of foliage cut a sharp V of green and gold against the azure of an unclouded sky, while the varied call and whistle of birds kept up a continuous echo of melody. Whoever it was who gave rise to the saying that South African birds have no song is guilty of libel, for the varying and melodious cheeriness of the bird voices, at any rate in bush country, constitutes one of its greatest charms, and the very unfamiliarity of these is in effective keeping with the wildness of the surroundings.

"Well, for some little time, at any rate," I answered.

"I'm glad. You're rather a good chap, you know, Mr Holt."

Beryl and I exchanged glances, she intensely amused, while I laughed outright.

"I didn't know it, Iris; but am delighted to learn the fact on your indisputable authority," I answered.

She flung a handful of grass sprays at me, which she had been absently plucking.

"Don't use those beastly long words," she said. "No, but really I am glad."

The straight glance of the pretty blue eyes full upon my face expressed all a delightful child's genuine liking. I own to having felt in my innermost self considerably moved thereby.

"I must take off my hat this time," I said, suiting the action to the word with a sweep of mock elaboration. "Miss Matterson, will you second the resolution just proposed?" I added, turning to Beryl.

"Ah, why do you always say 'Miss Matterson'?" interrupted Iris decisively. "It's so stiff. Why don't you say 'Beryl'?"

"May I?" was the obvious rejoinder—indeed, the only possible one.

"Why not, Mr Holt? I'm sure if there is anybody whom we have every reason to look upon as one of ourselves it is you." Yet with the words, frank and friendly as they were, ever so slight a colour had come into the sweet calm face. But before I could make any reply Iris emitted a loud whistle.

"Look at that, Beryl," she cried derisively. "And then you call him 'Mr Holt.'"

"The very thing I was going to remark upon," I said.

"Very well, then," said Beryl. "Then I won't do it again." This time the colour had disappeared, but I could have sworn I caught a momentary look in those soulful eyes that would have justified me, had I been alone, in throwing my hat in the air and hooraying, or executing any other frantic and maniacal manoeuvre indicative of delirious exaltation.

"Then it's a bargain," I said.

"Yes," smiled Beryl.

Now what had given rise to that dear child's original remark was a certain conversation that had been held that morning over at the kraals at counting-out time.

"Why don't you make up your mind to stop out here altogether, Holt?" Brian had said, as, the job aforesaid over, we were leaning against a gate watching the flocks streaming away to their respective pasture grounds. "You seem to take to the life, too. Man, you'll never feel at home in one of those beastly stuffy offices again after this, grinding away at figures. Why don't you cut loose from it all, and fix up out here? You can do it. Don't you think he ought, dad?"

"I think he might do worse," was the answer. "As you say, he seems to take readily enough to it."

With the words an idea had flashed into my brain, an idea that was as a veritable illumination.

"But before I could start on my own account I should want a precious deal more experience than I've got at present," I said. "There are heaps of things I should have to learn."

"Yes, you would have a good deal to learn," said Septimus Matterson, shading a match with his hands as he lit his pipe.

"Look here, Mr Matterson," I said, coming straight to the point. "Will you teach me—you and Brian? I am not a man of large means, but anything in the way of a premium that you may think fair, I shall be only too happy—er—er—that I am content to leave entirely to you," I stuttered.

Septimus Matterson had lit his pipe now, and stood emitting puffs of smoke slowly, while a queer smile deepened upon his strong handsome face. Then he said—

"I don't often swear, Holt, as I believe you'll bear me out in saying. But in this case I'm going to make an exception. Premium be damned!"

At this Brian threw back his head and roared, while I, puzzled, grinned idiotically.

"What I mean is," he went on, "in the first place it's not likely I'd take any remuneration from you for giving me a helping hand. Even if you hadn't saved my darling little girl's life, as a friend of Brian's you're heartily welcome to any assistance I could give you. Wait a bit—" interrupting the protest I was trying to stammer forth. "In the next place, we don't as a rule take premiums in this country for teaching a fellow to farm—the few who do are generally just the ones who can't teach him anything at all. And, finally, every word I said to you the other day I meant. So if you're inclined to stay on here and pick up your knowledge of the life and experience of the country by helping us, why this place is your home for just as long as ever you like to make it so."

"Rather," appended Brian in his quietly emphatic way. "Give us a fill, dad," reaching out a hand for the paternal pouch.

I have but a confused idea of what I said in reply, probably something incoherent, as my way is when genuinely moved, possibly because that is a mental process I so seldom undergo. Anyhow, the matter was settled to the satisfaction of all parties, which was the main thing.

Chapter Eleven.

The Objectionable Trask.

Now as I sat there, that still and radiant afternoon, in the sylvan wildness of our shaded resting-place, whose cool gloom contrasted well with the golden warmth of the sunlight beyond, I was rather more disposed for silence than speech. I was thinking, and the subject matter of my thoughts was all unalloyed with any misgiving of foreboding that should tarnish its brightness. I was realising Beryl's presence, and all that it meant to me. There she was, within a couple of yards of me, and the mere consciousness of this was all-sufficing. I was contrasting, too, this wondrous change which had come into my life—such a joy of living, such a new awakening to its possibilities. It seemed I was hardly the same man. I who had hitherto gone through life in a neutral-tinted sort of way, content to exist from day to day among neutral-tinted surroundings, with, as I thought hitherto, a happy immunity from all violent interests or emotions. And now, by an almost magical wave of a wizard wand, I had been transported to this fair land, to sunlight from gloom, to a golden awakening from a drab slumbrous acquiescence in a bovine state of existence, which supplied the physical wants, leaving all others untouched. And the magic which had wrought this upheaval—

"Well? A penny for your thoughts."

I turned to the speaker. It was perhaps as well that the child was with us, or I don't know what I might have been led into saying, probably prematurely, and would thus have tumbled down my own bright castles in the air.

"He's thinking of his pipe," said Iris mischievously. "Brian always gets into a brown study too when he's plunged in smoke. Beryl, I think we must make him put it out."

"Don't be a little barbarian, Iris," I answered, knocking the ashes out of the offending implement. "The fact is, I was thinking of what a blessed instrument of Providence was the prow of the *Kittiwake* when it knocked my sculling boat to matchwood in mid-Channel and brought me here. That was all."

"Oh yes. You were thinking you'd like to be back in that smoky old London of yours, and how slow we all are," retorted Iris. "Trask's always crowding London down our throats. I hate the very sound of its name. It must be a beastly hole. I always ask him why he doesn't go back there if he's so fond of it."

"I should say *Mr* Trask, Iris," I said, with a sly glance at Beryl.

"Ach!" exclaimed the child disgustedly, throwing a handful of grass stalks at me.

After all, we were only enjoying a lazy Sunday afternoon, talking nonsense, as people will at such times—anyhow, indulging in no rational conversation worth chronicling. And Beryl and I would engage in a playful argument on some unimportant trifle, and Iris, with child-like restlessness, would wander about, now throwing a stone into a water-hole to scare a mud turtle floating with its head on the surface, or peer about from bush to bush trying to discover a bird's nest; and at last as the afternoon wore on we started to retrace our steps homeward.

It will always linger in my memory, that peaceful, utterly uneventful stroll. The flaming wheel of the westering sun was drawing down to the farther ridge as we came in sight of the tree-embowered homestead, with a soft blue smoke-reek or two curling up into the still air. The bleat of the returning flocks was borne to us from the distance; and, approaching along a bush path which should converge with ours, came half a dozen Kafirs of both sexes, walking single file, the red ochre colouring their blankets and persons harmonising not uneffectively with the prevailing green of the surroundings, while the full tones of their melodious language—the deep bass of the males and the rich pleasing inflection of women's voices as they conversed—added an additional note of completeness to the closing beauty of a typical African day. And within my mind was the all-pervading thought that this day was but the beginning of many such; that the next, and the morrow, and the day after, that would be brightened and illuminated by the same sweet companionship—even that of her who was now beside me; that each day's occupation would be sweetened and hallowed by the thought that we were dwellers beneath the same roof—and then—and then—who could tell? Ah, it was one of those periods that come to some of us at a time in our lives when imagination is fresh, and heart and mind unseared by shattered illusions, and the corroding gall of latter days not even so much as suspected then.

"Hullo!" I exclaimed, catching sight of a third figure strolling beside Brian and his father, "Who's that? Looks like Trask."

"Yes, it is," assented Beryl.

The appearance of the stranger seemed to mar the harmony of the situation to my mind. I did not like Trask. He was one of those men who, wherever they find themselves, never give any one a chance of forgetting their presence; no, not even for a moment. When Trask appeared at Gonya's Kloof—which, by the way, was the name of the Mattersons' farm—why, there was no possibility of overlooking the fact, for he simply monopolised the whole conversation. He was a man of about my own height and build, and three or four years my senior, on the strength of which, and of having about that amount of colonial experience, he chose to assume towards my humble self a good-humouredly contemptuous and patronising manner, which to me was insufferable. Not infrequently, too, he would try his hand at making me a butt for his exceedingly forced and laboured wit, which is a thing I don't take. He was a neighbour of twelve miles or so, where he farmed—or was supposed to farm—his own place, and was reputed well off. To crown his other offences in my eyes, he was a bachelor, and was a precious deal too fond of coming over to Gonya's Kloof on any or no pretext.

Turning from his greeting to the girls—a greeting to my mind dashed with a perfectly unwarrantable tone of familiarity—he opened on me.

"Ha, Holt, getting more into the way of things now, I suppose? You'll soon know your way about. Things take a little getting into at first—ha-ha!"

This in a sort of bray, accompanied by a condescending expression.

Catching Brian's eye, I discerned a killing twinkle therein.

"Why, Trask," he said in his quiet way, "Holt's got into the way of things about twice as quick as any imported man I ever knew."

"Yes. Twice as quick," repeated Beryl, in emphatic assent.

I fancy Trask didn't like this—he looked as if he didn't; but I did, though of course I made no sign either way. Now all this was petty, and by every rule I ought to have been superior to any such trivial annoyances. But bear in mind that I make no claim to be a hero; indeed, I propose in this narrative to set down my own weaknesses with a candid and impartial hand. And I intensely disliked Trask.

The latter proceeded to make himself at home. Of course he was going to stay the evening, equally of course when we sat down to table he must needs plant himself on the other side of Beryl, and the only thing that kept him from entirely monopolising her was that he could not bring himself to allow the attention of any one else in the room to stray for many moments from himself, and as usual the conversation consisted of Trask, with an occasional monosyllable of assent or dissent interjected elsewhere. So hidebound was the self-complacency of Trask that even George found it profitless to cheek him with any effect, although in justice to George I am bound to say he tried his level best.

"What stay are you making, Holt?" brought out Trask, by way of varying the conversation.

Now this sort of query propounded to a guest right in the eye of his entertainers has always struck me as the very acme of idiotic tactlessness, and about on a par with asking an acquaintance of twenty minutes' standing whether he's married. Yet nothing is more common to encounter than both forms of foolishness. But before I could frame an adequate reply Brian answered for me.

"He's staying on altogether, Trask. We're going to put him up to the ropes."

"Eh? Altogether? What? Going to fix up in this country then?"

I nodded, for I could not speak. I had just caught Brian's eye, and the expression therein was too much for my feelings. I should have exploded had I attempted speech, for the blank astonishment on Trask's face was too comical. He looked about as happy under the announcement as though somebody had just begun to open fire upon him with shrapnel. But he said something about "the more the merrier," which, I fear, was not a genuine expression of sentiment in the present instance.

"Pass the quince jam, please, Kenrick."

Clear and unconcerned rose Iris' voice. Every one stared, while Brian emitted a subdued whistle.

"Hullo, young woman, you're getting on," he said.

The little girl grinned with mischievous delight, showing two extremely pretty rows of white teeth.

"Oh, it's all right," she said. "We've arranged all that. He's my big brother now, hey, Kenrick?"

"Why, certainly," I confirmed gravely, but with more inward merriment over Trask's expression of countenance. Indeed, the possible implication conveyed by the statement was calculated to evolve some sensation all round. Even Brian looked puzzled for a moment, but only for a moment.

"And when did you confer that supreme honour upon him, Iris?" he said.

"This afternoon. He's much too good a chap to go on mistering him," answered this impudent child, with a decisive nod of her pretty head. "Anyhow, we're not going to do it, are we, Beryl?"

"I say, Iris, you're making me blush like the mischief, you know," I put in. "Well, it's consoling to know that one's trumpeter isn't dead."

"Ha-ha-ha! May I ask, Miss Matterson, whether you are included in this newly formed—ha—fraternity?" said Trask in his most asinine tones; but then he was always a tactless fool.

"Call it the Confraternity of the Shipwrecked Mariners," said Brian, possibly in order to save Beryl the trouble of answering the idiotic question. And as though to render the diversion more complete still, something between an exclamation and a groan escaped from the master of the house at the other end of the table.

"Why, what is it, father?" cried Beryl, half starting up in alarm.

"Nothing, dear. Only this confounded rheumatism. Am all ache from head to foot. Sharper twinge than usual—couldn't help singing out. Must have caught a chill on top of it."

"Father, you must go to bed at once," said Beryl decisively. "Brian and I will come and look after you."

"Well, I think I will. Good-night everybody. Trask, you'll excuse me."

Septimus Matterson was, as he said, anything but well, and his early retirement rather put a damper on the evening from Trask's point of view, especially as Beryl was out of the room looking after her father. Moreover, Trask prided himself on his capacity for singing comic songs, which he accompanied himself, and, to give the devil his due, uncommonly well. But under the circumstances there was no demand for this form of entertainment to-night, and it was rather earlier than usual when we found ourselves alone together, he and I, for he had needed no pressure to be induced to stay the night, and had been allotted a shakedown in the same room with me.

Now, Trask was one of those men—of whom there are plenty, and women too—who are entirely different when there is no gallery to play to; in a word, Trask alone with one was entirely different to Trask showing off before a crowd, and in fact might have been taken for an ordinarily decent fellow, before you became alive to a little trick he had of engaging you in what would seem at the time quite an interesting conversation or discussion, only to reproduce with variations any idea you might so have expressed, in order to turn you into ridicule when he should next get an audience. But I, who had already experienced this idiosyncrasy, confined conversation with its exploiter to the merest commonplace, wherefore conversation soon languished. Trask was asleep, and I was just drowsing off, when a tap at the door and Brian's voice started me wide awake again.

"What's the row? Anything wrong?" I said.

"Wrong? Yes, very much wrong," was the answer, and striking a match he proceeded to light my candle.

Chapter Twelve.

Pursuit.

"The Kafirs have walked off the whole of the *bonte* span and three horses," went on Brian.

"Is that all?" I said, intensely relieved.

"That all? Man alive! but those are our best trek oxen. A full span of sixteen. 'That all'!"

"Oh, I don't mean it that way. My first thought was that your father was worse. You know how seedy he was this evening."

"I see!" was the answer. "No, he's no worse—fast asleep, in fact. I wouldn't disturb him about this, but—Holt, we must go after them at once."

"Go after who?" interrupted Trask, sitting up and yawning, for we had been talking in a low tone and he had not awoke at once. "What's the row, anyhow?"

Brian repeated what he had just been telling me. "The cheek of the brutes!" he went on. "Mind, this thing was done in broad daylight. I suppose they thought that as it was Sunday none of us would be about. Dumela came upon the fresh spoor as he was out looking after that sick cow down in the kloof by Aasvogel Krautz. They simply collected them, and swept off the lot. In broad daylight, too."

"I'm your man, Matterson," said Trask, briskly, having nearly got into his clothes. "I'll take a hand in this game."

"Thanks. I was going to ask you. George and Kleinbooi are getting up the horses now. We must start as soon as ever they are here."

"What gees have the niggers taken, Brian?" I asked.

"Why, Beryl's horse, Meerkat, for one, the bay colt, and the third's uncertain."

Beryl's horse! Here was an additional incentive to the undertaking, I thought.

"Dumela spoored them easily to Sand Drift," went on Brian, "and then it got too dark. If the old fool had come straight back at once and told us, we should have saved several hours; but not he. One of Stoffel Pexter's people told him they'd seen three mounted Kafirs and two on foot go through just above the drift with a span of large *bonte* oxen. So we'd better go straight there and start on the spoor from there. One thing, we can't miss it. It's as broad as a waggon road."

"Think they'll show fight if we come up with them, Brian?" I said.

"Don't know. We'll take our guns in case of accidents. John Kafir has more respect for an armed crowd than for an unarmed one. Now—if you fellows are ready, we'll lose no time getting under way. They are bringing up the horses now," as a trampling was heard without. "Put a few extra cartridges in your pocket, Holt, while I find a shooter for Trask."

I came out on the stoep and—from another door so did Beryl.

"It's too bad to rout you out of bed to start off like this on a midnight foray," she said.

The other two were inside, presumably arming. The fresh cool breaths of the midnight veldt, the circumstance of our projected undertaking, the knowledge that I was in a way rendering personal service to her who stood there, lent a curious dash of excitement and romance to the situation. The air was sharp, and the wrapper which she had thrown over her head framed and set forth the calm sweet face, and the lustrous eyes seemed to take on a softer expression in the starlight. I believe I nearly made a fool of myself then and there.

"Too bad?" I echoed. "Why, I would not have missed this for anything; especially as it holds out the additional attraction of being able to do something for you in particular."

She looked puzzled. "For me in particular," she repeated wonderingly. Then with the flash of a smile, "No, I give it up. Explain."

"To recover your horse."

"Who, Meerkat? Have they stolen him, then? Brian—" as the other two now reappeared, "you never told me that Meerkat was one of the horses that are gone."

"Oh, hang it! I've let the cat out of the bag," I said disgustedly. "I ought to kick myself."

"Don't do that. Bring back Meerkat instead," said Beryl, in her sweet, even way.

Of course I pledged myself to do so or die in the attempt, and all the rest of it—but my protestations were ruthlessly broken in upon by Brian's voice. Brian has a brisk, healthy decisiveness about him when carrying out any responsible matter, which seldom fails to secure attention, wherefore now his reminder that it was time to start was effectual in cutting my farewells rather short.

"Man, I wish I was going," said George grumpily, as he watched us mount. "It's a beastly shame I can't."

Nobody took any notice of this, but Trask must needs sing out—

"So long, Miss Matterson. We'll bring back the spoil, never fear."

"Oh, great Caesar!" said Brian. "Why don't you blow a trumpet while you're about it, Trask—or fire a few shots by way of letting the whole countryside know we're on the move?"

Decidedly Brian was in a "commandeering" vein. But the reproof was deserved.

Yes, it was exciting, that midnight going forth—exciting and enjoyable, as we moved on through the gloom, now riding abreast and talking, though in a low tone, as to the chances that lay before us, now falling into single file as our way narrowed into a cattle track through the bush. A brief off-saddle, then on again, and just as the first suspicion of dawn appeared in the east we descended a steep rocky path into a river valley. A Dutch farmhouse, rough of aspect, stood on an open space beyond the drift, and hard by it a few tumble-down sheep kraals and two or three native huts.

"That's all right," said Brian, having satisfied himself as to the identity of three human figures engaged in converse in front of the house. "Revell has been able to come. I was afraid Dumela wouldn't find him at home."

We rode through the drift, which was very low at that time of year, and as we dismounted I saw before me a swarthy Dutchman—who was the Stoffel Pexter before alluded to; an Englishman, whose hair and beard simply flamed at you, so fiery and red were both—this was Revell; the third, a Kafir, being, in fact, old Dumela, our cattle herd.

"*Daag*, Matterson," began Pexter. "Are you on the spoor of your oxen? One of my *zwaartgoed* told me he'd seen them go through last night, so they've got a good start. He says it isn't Kuliso's schepsels this time—more likely Mpandhlile's."

"Likely. But let's have some coffee, Stoffel, for we've only half an hour to off-saddle—not a minute more," returned Brian decisively. "Awful good of you to turn out, Revell. Hardly expected to find you at home."

"Man, that's nothing," said the other, whom I had met before, and who albeit a bit rough was rather a good fellow. His weakness was an intense susceptibility as to the "warmth" of his summit, and he had been known to thrash more than one of his Kafirs to an unmerciful degree simply by reason of overhearing the use among them of his native name, "Ibomvu" (red). "Why, what'd we do in a country like this if we didn't turn out and help each other? Eh, Holt?"

"That's so," I answered; and now we adjourned to the house where Stoffel Pexter's *vrouw* had laid out cups of scalding hot coffee and *koekjes*. The worthy Boer was exceedingly cordial towards us, for the expedition we were on appealed more than anything to his sympathies, and to those of his class. The same thing might happen to himself at any time. The Kafirs were thieving, murdering dogs in his estimation, not a shade better than wild beasts—in short, our natural enemies. So he wished us every success; and further, pressed upon us a bag of biltong, which he thought might come in handy before we got back. And we thought so too.

We took up the spoor at the place where the stolen animals were seen to cross the river. It was indeed as broad as a waggon road, as Brian had predicted, even to a tyro such as myself, for the ground was studded with fresh hoof marks; but the marauders were evidently old hands at the game, for avoiding steep hills which might blow the animals, they had made use of a narrow cattle track winding along through a deep rugged ravine, but ever ascending. We, however, had managed to travel much faster, and very soon halted to blow the horses on the heights overlooking the river valley, where, like a toy house in the distance, we could see the dwelling we had recently left. Here we came up with Dumela, who had started on ahead, and had made the distance in most excellent time.

Now we commanded a new view of country. Before us unfolded a panorama of wide rolling plain and bushy kloof, stretching away to further heights— dark, forest-clad and beautiful—but, on our then errand, forbidding. At these Dumela gazed fixedly, as he said, in his roundabout native way—

"Only if they are strong enough to keep it do those who steal an ox flaunt its skin in everybody's face. It is there you will find the oxen."

"How do you know that, Dumela?" said the irrepressible Trask, in Dutch, when this had been translated to us. The Kafir grinned with, I thought, a touch of contempt, and which wholly amused Brian, as he muttered to himself—

"Some white people are like women—always asking things they ought to know." But out loud he said: "Why should I deceive you? I have nothing to gain by the oxen being stolen. They are my master's—that is, *mine*; for they were under my care."

Dumela was to leave us here, but before he started upon his homeward way, he said to Brian, "*Inkose*, you will find what you seek, but whether you will obtain possession of it, I know not, for the people over yonder are numerous and fierce and reckless, and they love not the whites—wherefore keep your eyes open."

"That's the dickey part of the whole situation," said Brian, as we moved forward. "If we come to blows and had a free hand, why we'd probably be all right. As it is, it's like fighting with one hand tied behind you. There's no actual war on—not yet—though if things go on much longer like this there soon will be. If we start shooting to kill—or even shooting at all—ten to one it means a Circuit Court trial; but if they cut all our throats, not one of them'll be any the worse for it—for even if the right men were ever dropped upon, it would be ruled that they acted in self-defence, and that armed parties of farmers had no right raiding into native locations."

"Quite right, Matterson," assented Revell. "They'd jaw about taking the law into our own hands, and what did the Colony keep up an expensive Police Force for, and so on. Fat lot you'd see of your oxen by the time you put that machinery to work. Why, the Kafirs'd have scoffed the whole span long before and started out to rake in more."

Now, all this was no more than the bare truth. The unrest and bold and predatory propensities of our turbulent neighbours of late had been the cause of a growing uneasiness on the frontier, and more than one armed collision between settlers and the natives had occurred—arising out of just such provocation as had brought us hither. One indeed, quite recently, had been something of a *cause célèbre* in that to the frantic indignation of the presiding judge a frontier jury had unhesitatingly and obstinately refused to convict certain individuals of their own class and colour who had used fire-arms with fatal effect, but beyond all doubt in defence of their own lives.

"We may find ourselves in a rotten tight place, or we may not," pronounced Brian, when we had discussed the whole position fore and aft. "If we do we must use judgment, and on no account loose off a shot unless we are absolutely and unequivocally obliged. Is that understood, you fellows?"

"Certainly," was the answer on the part of myself and Revell. But Trask was not so unanimous.

"Do you mean to say, Matterson, that I'm to let a nigger cut my throat before I pull trigger on him? Because if so, I'm lowed if I do, and that's all about it," he said.

There was a queer look in Brian's face as he answered—

"I mean to say nothing so idiotic. But, all things considered, Trask, perhaps you'll oblige me by going home, and leaving us three to straighten out this worry. Now do. We shall get on so much better that way."

"What the very devil do you mean, Matterson?" blustered Trask.

"What I say—no more, no less. I'm bossing this undertaking. I'm obliged to you for volunteering, but if you think you've got a better plan than mine, why we shan't get on. That's all."

"Oh, blazes, man. I didn't mean that. I'll do anything you like," answered Trask, after a moment's hesitation, during which all hands thought the row might end in blows. "I'm not going to turn tail and go back now—not much."

"It's no question of turning tail, but of using ordinary and sound judgment," rejoined Brian. "We shall be glad enough of your help on those terms."

"Oh, all right, old chap. Say no more about it," conceded the other with a sort of bluff, would-be good-natured growl—and the difference thus patched up, we resumed our way.

But I, in my heart of hearts, most devoutly wished we were through with it, for in marching into the nest of fierce and truculent barbarians which was our objective, it seemed to me we were placing ourselves between the very sharp horns of a bad dilemma. In sheer savagery, and trusting in the immunity which a paternal Government would be sure to extend to them, the sportive barbarians aforesaid might incontinently massacre the lot of us, or, if in defending ourselves any of our enemies got hurt, why then under the laws of our country we might have to stand our trial for murder. But the third solution of the difficulty, that we should return with whole skins and clean hands, and that for which we had come out, viz., the recovered stock, seemed to me just then rather too good to be hoped for.

Chapter Thirteen.

Checked.

For some hours we held on without difficulty. It became very hot. The sun's rays poured down into the close, shut-in kloofs as from the lens of a gigantic burning-glass; and the atmosphere was unmoved by a single puff of wind. The horses were in a bath of perspiration, and it became evident they must be off-saddled, wherefore a halt was called in a cool, shady place, where they could enjoy to the full a much-needed rest. It was a bushy secluded spot beneath an overhanging cliff, from whose face a whole cloud of spreuws flashed hither and thither, whistling in lively alarm, but, best of all, it contained a cool clear water-hole, albeit the liquid was slightly brackish.

"Tired, Holt?" asked Brian good-naturedly, as having knee-haltered the horses, we were discussing some supplies which had been brought in a saddle-bag. "Have a drop of grog."

"To the first I answer 'No,' to the second, 'Yes,' emphatically!" I said, catching the flask which he chucked across to me. It was a roomy metal one, with considerable carrying capacity.

"Well, this sort of forced march on an African summer day isn't a cool and invigorating promenade," cut in Trask. "After you, Holt."

We had a tot all round and a smoke. Then it became time to move on again. Once a check occurred, where the thieves had manifestly separated their spoil, but the device was only a blind, and soon solved by such experienced frontiersmen as Brian and Revell. Now and again we would sight a farmhouse, with its cultivated strip of mealie land, picturesquely nestling in some bushy hollow, but such we purposely avoided, for news travels on winged feet among Kafirs, and the arrival of an armed party at one of these homesteads would be extremely likely to be notified by any of the hangers-on there to their brethren of the marauding clans inhabiting the dark, frowning fastnesses which now began to rise not far in front. Nor was there any need to ask for information, for the spoor was as plain as plain could be, and soon, after leading us up a steep hillside, it suddenly left the bush, and, cresting the ridge, struck out into an open plain, where, a few hundred yards in front stood a large native kraal, the dark forms of whose inhabitants we could see moving about among the beehive-shaped huts. But the simultaneous yell and rush of a lot of curs promptly turned the attention of the said inhabitants upon us. It looked as if our appearance had been provocative of more than ordinary excitement.

"Don't shoot, Trask," said Brian warningly, observing that that worthy was aiming at a couple of large, mouthing curs whom he considered in rather too close proximity to his horse's hocks. "Don't shoot. We haven't time to stop and have a row here."

"Who is your headman?" he asked the half-dozen sullen, stalwart savages who had slouched forward to meet us.

"He is not here, *Umlúngu*," was the ready reply.

"*Who* is he, not *where* is he?" repeated Brian.

"He is away," again answered the man, a tall, grizzled Kafir with an evil expression of countenance.

"Now look," said Brian forcibly. "When did those oxen and horses pass by here? The spoor is at your very doors. One of you must go with us and carry it on, or you are responsible equally with the thieves."

By this time quite a number of Kafirs had come forth from among the huts by twos and threes, and were clustering around, a proportion armed with tough, heavy kerries, and their demeanour was sullen and unfriendly to a degree, as they muttered among themselves in their deep bass tones. Women, too, had raised their greasy, scantily-clad forms where they had been lolling against the huts basking in the sun with their round-headed, beady-eyed brats, and were gazing at us; the while discussing us with the freedom of their sex and in no flattering terms.

"*Au*! We know nothing about thieves, *Umlúngu*," replied the spokesman. "If any oxen came by here they did not stay here. Why not follow them further if you have followed them so far? Why trouble us?" And a great jeering guffaw greeted the words.

"Good," said Brian. "These oxen have been stolen, and we have traced them to the gates of your kraal. You will hear a great deal more about this."

"*Whau*!" exclaimed the savage, turning his back upon us. "Go. Go and find your oxen."

Again that insolent jeering laugh went up from the onlookers, and here an unpleasant discovery forced itself upon us. By accident or design, the crowd, which was now considerable, had closed round us on every side. A serried mass of dark, musky bodies, and grim—and it seemed threatening—faces walled us in, while requests for tobacco and other things were hurled at us in tones that savoured more of demand than petition. The aim of the savages was clear. They intended to delay our advance as long as possible. We had, rather foolishly, allowed ourselves to be led into a trap.

Then occurred the unexpected. A tall Kafir, in the forefront of the mob, pointing suddenly at Revell, ejaculated in great jeering tone—

"*Hau! Ibomvu!*"

And the shout ran through the whole crowd.

"*Ibomvu!*" roared the men. "*Yau! Ibomvu!*" shrilled the women in the background.

I have said something as to the effect produced upon our comrade by any allusion to his flaming poll. It seemed to drive him quite mad. It mattered not that it was uttered by one man or a thousand, the effect upon him was just the same, and this held good here. In less than a second he had put his horse straight at the original offender, and with a tough seacow-hide sjambok which dangled from his wrist was cutting into that astonished and ill-advised ruffian with the fury of a madman. On head and face and naked shoulders the terrible lash descended, and the lightning-like celerity of the attack was such as to leave neither time nor thought for resistance—the victim's one idea—if he had even one—being to escape from that awful lash, while those around, appalled by the white, infuriated countenance, and the frenzied plunging of the horse, gave way, though not before several of them had tasted the infliction; for Revell cut impartially right and left as though he were hewing his way through with a sabre. And in effect this is just what he might have been doing, for the crowd on that side opened out in wildest confusion, of which we took advantage, and in less than a minute were a couple of hundred yards from the spot.

And now a terrific hubbub arose in our rear. A glance over our shoulders showed the crowd roaring forward on our track, while among others who had dived into the huts to arm, we could see the bright gleam of assegais.

"Face round," cried Brian, "and aim, but for your lives don't fire. If we can't scare them to a halt we must turn and run. But—no shooting."

We wrenched our horses round. The roaring, surging rush of oncoming savages poured forward, then stopped. Four gun barrels sending forth their contents into the thick of the mob would create awful havoc, and there were four more in reserve, for we each had double barrels. Besides, they knew we could gallop out of reach at no loss to ourselves. So they halted, brandishing sticks and assegais, and howling out every kind of taunting and abusive epithet.

"*Ibomvu! Yau! Ibomvu!*" yelled Revell, in return, making his sjambok whistle through the air as he flourished it round his head. "Come on, all of you, and taste this. I'll cut the whole lot of you to thongs! I'll show you how *Ibomvu* can burn!"

This speech, in Kafir, raised another roar of menace and defiance, but the savages were not inclined to accept the invitation therein embodied, wherefore we turned our horses' heads, and proceeded leisurely onward.

"Go on, go on," howled the mob after us. "Go and find your oxen! They— up yonder—will know how to talk with you."

No further interruption occurred, and before us lay the tell-tale track, as clear as need be. At length the wooded heights rose immediately in front, and we halted for another short off-saddle.

"Now look here," began Brian, throwing himself on the ground, and filling his pipe. "It's evident these chaps don't care whether we follow them or not, but I believe we shall come up with them this evening, and we shall have a little over three hours of daylight to do it in. The sort of treatment we met with just now is a good earnest of what we've got to expect. And there are only four of us."

"Hooray for a row!" cried Trask.

"Yes, but we don't want a row if it can possibly be avoided. We're between the devil and the deep sea, which for present purposes may be taken to mean that none of us must fire a shot unless our lives depend upon it, and then, if possible, fire blank."

This oration was interrupted, and that by a thud of approaching hoof strokes and a sound of deep voices and laughter. A track wound round the hillside lower down, and we saw about a score of mounted Kafirs sweep past, chattering and laughing at the top of their voices. It was clear that this gang was returning from a visit to some canteen, for the condition of more than one of their number was not a little precarious, swaying and lurching in their ragged saddles as they belaboured their wretched undersized steeds.

"All as drunk as pigs," whispered Revell. "By George! That looks like Kuliso."

A tall, finely-made man, clad in an ancient pair of trousers and a red blanket and wearing an ivory ring on his left arm rode at the head of the gang, evidently a chief, for he was rather more drunk than the rest, and seemed to occupy a greater share of attention.

"No, it isn't," returned Brian. "I don't know who it is, though." And in a trice the weird equestrians, their red blankets streaming behind them, were whirled out of sight, and having given them time to get further on their way, we resumed our own.

There was nothing in itself gloomy or forbidding in the series of densely-wooded heights which now rose in front of us. Peaceful solitude rather than lurking danger was the idea conveyed by that winding succession of deep valleys and lofty hills slumbering in the golden light of the waning afternoon, yet the network of rugged ravines we were about to penetrate had, in former times, been the scene of more than one bloody encounter wherein the advantages had all lain with the wild denizens of the place. Many a dark episode could those tangled glens have told, of patrols surprised and outnumbered in the thick bush, of brave men struck down by the assegai of the savage, or dragged off, wounded and disabled, to be put to a lingering death of torture. Even at that time the locality held an evil repute as the haunt of cattle thieves and desperate characters generally.

We crossed a kind of deep basin shut in on all sides by wooded hills, then through a narrow *poort* overhung by aloe-fringed krantzes widening out into just such another basin. In fact, we seemed to have got into a veritable labyrinth of such—and through my own mind, at any rate, passed the thought—How were we going to get out? Then the clamour of dogs in front, and we suddenly came upon a kraal.

"Straight on," said Brian. "We can't stop. No time to waste."

The inhabitants gave us rather a sullen greeting, but made no demonstration, staring after us in lowering silence. And now the way became wilder and more rugged still, and the spoor, yet plain as ever, led us far down into a jungly glade, where the monkey ladders hung like trellis work from the twisted limbs of great yellow-wood trees, and here in the shaded gloom of the forest—for this was no mere scrub, but real forest—night seemed already to be drawing in.

"What's this?" said Brian, turning in his saddle to look back, as a long shrill cry arose in the distance, from the direction of the kraal we had left behind us.

"I hope they are not raising the country on our heels."

We paused and listened. The sound was repeated, far away behind us.

"Well, we must take our chance. 'Push on' is the word."

For some time we rode on in silence, over the same sort of ground as I have already described. And now the sky was glowing with blades of golden effulgence, as the rays of the declining sun lengthened, touching for a moment the face of a great iron-bound krantz starting up, here and there, from the dark impenetrable bush. A pair of crimson-winged louris darted across our path, but otherwise sign of life was there none. Somehow we felt that we must be very close upon the marauders, who might number ten or a hundred. Every moment had become one of tense excitement and expectation.

Chapter Fourteen.

An Overhaul.

"Magtig!" exclaimed Revell, "I swear I smell something roasting."

"S-s-s-h!" warned Brian, crouching low on his horse's neck. "Dismount, every one."

A few hundred yards beneath we now saw a kraal. It lay in a deep natural basin, walled in with rugged rocks and thick bush; but so shut in was it on all sides that this seemed the only way in or out. A curl of smoke rose into the still evening air, and the sound of several deep voices in conversation was plainly audible; and with it, the strong smell of roasting meat confirmed us in the certainty that we had at length reached the object of our quest; for Kafirs very rarely kill their own cattle, and this circumstance combined with the freshness of the spoor, left no further doubt in our minds.

And now, before we could formulate a plan, we heard a sound of trampling, and a number of oxen emerged from the thick bush beyond the kraal, urged forward by a single Kafir, who was driving them down to the gate of the thorn enclosure. There was no mistaking the large fine animals, white, but speckled all over with bluish black. It was Septimus Matterson's fine span.

"Wait—wait—wait!" whispered Brian, his voice in a tremble with excitement. "Let the devils bring them in—they are driving them right into our hands— and when I give the word, up and at them. We must charge right bang into them if there are five or five hundred. Down—keep down, Trask; they'll see your hat, man."

With straining eyes we watched the savages—for three or four more had joined the single driver—as they urged the stolen beasts down to the gate and stood on each side to pass them in. The animals having been driven fast and far that day, were disposed to give no trouble, but entered the enclosure quietly, one with another.

"Fifteen! They've killed one—and, by Jove! they are going to kill another," whispered Brian, as the Kafirs, shutting the kraal gate behind them, advanced towards one of the largest oxen with *reims* in their hands. "Now, are you all ready. We'll capture the fellows inside. Don't shout or anything but—up and at them!"

With a headlong rush we charged down upon the kraal, but the Kafirs had seen us. A loud warning cry, and several lithe dark forms bounded like cats over the fence, and half-running, half-creeping, made for the bush as fast as ever they could pelt, while three more who were seated round a fire, each with a beef bone in his fist, gnawing the meat off, flung it down among a heap of other relics of the feast, and started up to fly. Evidently they were unaware of the smallness of our force, or perhaps took us for a posse of Mounted Police.

"Look at that! Only look at that!" cried Revell, pointing to the fire, beside which lay the head and a remnant of the carcase of one of the stolen animals. And throwing all prudence to the winds, he up with his piece and let fly at one of the fleeing forms.

"Steady, steady!" warned Brian. "No shooting, mind! Trask, *do* you hear!"

Too late. Trask had already pressed the trigger, and more fortunate—or unfortunate—than Revell, who had missed, owing to the fidgeting of his horse, one of the fleeing Kafirs was seen to stumble and fall, then, rising with an effort, dragged himself into the welcome cover of the bush.

"First bird!" cried Trask, wild with excitement. "He's dead. I saw him 'tower.'"

"No, you didn't. You didn't see anything," returned Brian meaningly. "None of us saw anything of the sort, see! You only shot to scare, and I told you not to do that unless you were driven to it."

"That's so," said Revell, "we only shot to scare. Don't be an idiot, Trask."

"But—" began that obtuse worthy. "Oh—ah—um—yes, I see!" he broke off as the idea at last found lodgment in his thick skull.

Now all this had befallen in a very twinkling. The thieves had vanished as though into thin air—certainly into thick bush—and here we were, with fifteen out of the sixteen oxen composing the stolen span: better luck than might have fallen to our lot. But what about the stolen horses? And just then, as though in reply to my thoughts, I, who was taking no part in the foregoing wrangle, suddenly beheld two mounted figures dart away from some hiding place just the other side of the kraal. In a moment they were under cover of the bush and safe out of shot, but in that moment I had recognised the steed bestridden by the hindermost one. It was Meerkat—Beryl's own particular and favourite horse—and it I had pledged myself to recover.

Shouting my discovery to the others, I was off on the track of the fugitives, like a whirlwind. In that moment I recognised that none followed me. I heard, moreover, Brian's voice peremptorily ordering me back, but to it I turned a deaf ear, for still clearer seemed to sound Beryl's voice urging me forward. "Bring back Meerkat," had been her parting words to me. And now there the horse was—not so very far in front of me. Brian might shout himself voiceless: this time I would pay no attention to him. A mad gallop, a short exhilarating pursuit, I would knock off its back the greasy rascal who was riding it, and would bring back the horse—Beryl's horse—in triumph. The idea was more than exhilarating.

Yes, but behind that lay its realisation, and this was not quite so easy. For the way was literally "dark and slippery." Over staircase-like rocks, and rolling, slipping stones, it ran, now beneath the gloom of trees, now through lower scrub, whose boughs, flying back, more than once nearly swept me from the saddle. Listening intently, I could just catch the faint click of hoofs away in front, and with a sinking of heart I recognised that this sound seemed to be growing even more faint. The consciousness maddened me, and I spurred my faithful steed along that rugged way, plunging, floundering, but getting along somehow, in a manner not to be contemplated in cold blood.

If the path was damnable, the ascent was easy, luckily, though rugged. I gave no thought as to whether any of my comrades were following, or if I did it was only a jealous misgiving lest I should not be, the first to come up with the quarry. The thieves might escape, for all I cared; the other horse might not be recovered, but recapture Beryl's I would. Then I awoke to the unpleasing realisation that dusk was giving way to darkness, the downright sheer darkness of night.

All the more reason for bringing the undertaking to a swift conclusion: wherefore I pommelled and spurred my hapless steed along with a ruthlessness of which at any other time I should be heartily ashamed. But here the end justified the means, and soon I was rewarded, for I heard the click of hoofs much nearer ahead now, and with it the smothered tone of a voice or two.

Of course it should have occurred to me, had I not been transformed into a born idiot for the time being, that I was acting the part of one. For here I was, a man who had been little more than a month in the country, about to rush into the midst of unknown odds, to attack single-handed how many I knew not of fierce and savage desperadoes, right in their own especial haunt, in the thick of their own wild fastnesses; for it was highly probable that those whom I pursued had joined, or been joined by, others in front. Yet if I gave the matter a thought it was only a passing one.

Now my steed pricked up its ears and began to whinny, recognising the close propinquity of its friends, and there sure enough, as the bush thinned out somewhat, I could see the two runaways barely that number of hundred yards ahead. Putting on a spurt I had halved the distance, when they halted. He who bestrode Beryl's steed was an evil-looking savage with a string of blue beads about his neck, and an expression of contemptuous ferocity on his countenance as he faced round and awaited me, trying to conceal a long tapering assegai which he held ready to cast. But I rode straight for him, and when within thirty yards he launched the spear. Heavens! I could feel the draught created by the thing as it whizzed by my ear with almost the velocity of a bullet, and then I was upon him. But the fellow, who was quite a good horseman for a Kafir, managed to get hold of my bridle rein and, jerking it partly from my hand, hung back with it in such wise as to prevent my steed from ranging alongside of his. A mad, murderous temptation flashed through my mind to empty my shot barrel into his abominable carcase, but Brian's emphatic warning still in my memory availed to stay my hand.

I hardly know what happened then, or how. Whether it was that my horse, violently tugging backwards, succeeded in jerking the rein free, or my adversary, seeing his opportunity, had purposely let go, but the sudden recoil caused my fool of an animal to lose his balance and go clean over, taking me with him, and lo! I was rolling ignominiously upon the ground, though, fortunately, not under him. I saw the grin on the face of my late enemy, heard his jeering guffaw, and then—something swooped down over my head and shoulders shutting out sight and air in a most horrible and nauseous suffocation, pinning my arms to my sides, which several hands securely bound there. A babel of deep jeering voices filled my ears, muffled as they were, and I was seized and violently hustled forward at a great pace over a rough and stony way, the vicious dig of an assegai in my thigh emphasising a volley of injunctions which I could not understand. What I could understand, however, was that was expected to walk, and to walk smartly, too, guided by the very ungentle hands which urged me forward.

Chapter Fifteen.

The Den of the Cattle Stealers.

To give an adequate idea of my thoughts and feelings at that moment, or during those that followed, would amount to a sheer impossibility. Truly I had distinguished myself. I had undertaken to recover the stolen steed in bold and doughty fashion, and had allowed myself to be drawn into the most transparent booby-trap ever devised for the deception of mortal idiot. Instead of returning in triumph, having fulfilled Beryl's parting injunction, here was I, strapped up helplessly, my head and face swathed in a filthy greasy Kafir blanket, only able to breathe—and that with difficulty—through its unspeakably nauseous folds. Heavens! I wonder I was not sick. Kicked and punched too, and a butt for every kind of jeer and insult from these black ruffians, although of course I could not understand the burden of the latter. But where was it going to end?

Why had they not murdered me then and there? I thought. Could it be that they were taking me to some secure place where they might do it at their leisure, and hide away my body in some hole or cave where there was not the smallest chance of it ever being found, and so bearing witness against themselves? It looked like it—and the idea made my blood run cold with a very real and genuine fear.

All thoughts of rescue—of immediate rescue—I was forced to put aside; delayed rescue would be too late. My comrades would hardly succeed in spooring us in the dark, and it was quite dark now; moreover, they were but three, and judging from the varying voices of those who held me, the latter must be fairly numerous. No, the situation was hopeless—abjectly hopeless. Half-dead with fatigue and semi-suffocation, my mind a prey to the most acute humiliation and self-reproach, I stumbled on—how I did so I hardly know. At last I could bear it no longer. They might kill me if they liked, but not another step would I stir until that horrible suffocating gag was removed.

Something of this must have struck them too, for after a muttered consultation, they began fumbling at the cattle thongs with which I was bound, and lo; the filthy blanket was dragged off my head, and I sat drinking in the fresh night air in long draughts.

"No talk—no call out," said a voice at my side. "You talk—you call out, then—so."

It was not too dark to see the significant drawing of the hand across the speaker's throat by which the injunction was emphasised. The latter I judged it advisable to obey—for the present at any rate.

In this way we kept on through the night; it seemed to me for hours. I could make out the loom of the heights against the star-gemmed sky, and noticed that it narrowed considerably as though we were threading a long defile. More than once I stumbled, and not having the use of my hands to save myself, fell flat on my face, to the brutal amusement of the ruffians in whose power I was. I deemed it inadvisable to look about me too much, but could make out quite a dozen forms in front of me, and that there were plenty behind, I gathered from the hum of muffled voices. Indeed, another sense than that of sight went to confirm any conjecture as to their numbers, for the sweet night air was constantly poisoned by a reek of rancid grease and musky, foetid humanity. But of the three horses I could now see no sign.

At last a brief halt was made, evidently at some known water-hole or spring, for soon one of them emerged from the bush bearing a great calabash, and the sound of the splashing liquid as it was poured into bowls was as very music to my ears. The long, rough, forced march; the dash and excitement which had preceded it, had done their work. I was simply parched with thirst, and said so.

Thereupon the English-speaking Kafir came towards me with a smaller bowl. He put it to my lips, but before I could reach it the brute withdrew it again and dashed the contents into my face.

"That all the water you get," he laughed.

It was too much. Even the fear of immediate vengeance counted for nothing at that moment. My arms were secured but my legs were not. Throwing myself backward as I sat I let out with these in such wise as to plant both feet, with the force of a battering ram, right in the pit of the stomach of my jeering tormentor as he bent over me laughing. He rebounded like an indiarubber ball, rolled half a dozen yards, and lay writhing and groaning and gasping—while I, of course, made up my mind to instant death.

But to my surprise the other Kafirs seemed to think it the best joke in the world, for they burst out laughing immoderately, mocking and chaffing their damaged comrade, imitating him even, as he twisted and groaned in his agony. I remembered the saying that a crowd that laughs is not dangerous, and to that extent felt reassured. Yet, what when my victim should have recovered? That would be the time to look out for squalls.

Taking advantage of their good humour, I uttered the word "*Manzi.*" They stared; then one fellow got up and taking the calabash, shook it. Yes, there was still a little, and pouring it into a bowl brought it to me, letting me drink this time, he still shaking with laughter over the amusement I had just afforded them. Then we resumed our way.

This seemed to be along the steep side of a mountain, and judging from the increased freshness of the air we appeared to have gained a good altitude. Refreshed by my drink of water I was able to travel better, and I looked somewhat eagerly about, with an eye to possibilities, resolved, too, to keep one for any opportunity. On the one hand our way seemed overhung by cliffs; on the other, space. Finally the whole gang struck inward between what looked like narrowing rock walls, and came to a halt.

And now, as the fire which had been promptly started blazed up, I saw that our resting place was beneath a gigantic overhanging slab of rock, forming a sort of cave. Beyond this I could catch sight of a patch of stars with dark tree-tops waving gently against them; the while I was guided to the back of the recess, and bidden to sit down, an invitation I had no desire to dispute, after my late exertions. But they had, apparently, no idea of loosening the thongs, and my very superficial knowledge of their tongue did not rise to the point of requesting it. In sooth, I began to wish I had treated my erstwhile tormentor with a little less violence. I could have used him as a medium of conversation at any rate.

Now from some place of concealment was dragged forth a live sheep, tied by the legs; while one of the Kafirs was sharpening a butcher's knife upon a slab of rock. Poor beast! Its condition appealed to me in that mine was exactly similar, and the probabilities were that its fate would be mine, with the difference that I should not be eaten afterwards; for it was there and then butchered, and the flaying and quartering being accomplished in a surprisingly short space of time, the entire carcase was disposed by relays upon the glowing fire, and indeed the hissing and sputtering, and the odours of the roast, filled my own nostrils with a grateful savour. I could do with a mutton chop or two, after the scanty fare and hard exertion of the recent twelve hours.

Soon the feasting began, and there was a great chewing, and cracking of bones. The while I sat and endeavoured calmly to size up the whole situation. And its accessories were about as wild and grim as the most startling annals of any romance. Here was I, helpless, in the power and at the mercy of a score or so of as cut-throat a set of naked and ochre-smeared savages, as such romance could picture; forcibly brought here to this probably unknown fastness of theirs, and for what? From motives of self-preservation alone they could not afford to restore me to liberty after having once been in this, which was probably one of their most secure retreats, and I was conscious of a dire and terrible sinking of heart. Yet there was no war between ourselves and these people. They would hardly, therefore, go such lengths as to kill me, and so raise the whole countryside upon them. But as against this came another thought. There is no declared war between society and the dangerous and criminal classes in London or New York or Paris, or any other great city. Yet he who should venture into the innermost haunts of these and place himself in their power would be extremely unlikely ever to be seen again by inquiring friends; and my case here was precisely similar.

Recognising that a well-fed man is likely to be in better humour than a fasting one, be he savage or civilised, I waited until these had nearly finished their repast before intimating by signs and such few words as I knew, that I should like some small share of it. They stared, laughed, then one took a strip of meat from the fire, and came over to me, holding it up in a sort of bob-cherry fashion. But I was not to be taken in so easily as that, and uttered the word for hot. At this they laughed harder than ever, and having waited long enough, I soon got outside the mutton, hunger overcoming my repugnance to being fed in so unappetising, not to say disgusting, a fashion. But the whole episode seemed to put them into high good humour, from which I had begun to augur great things, when an interruption occurred which was inauspicious in the extreme. This was caused by a new arrival, none other than the evil-looking rascal whom I had rendered temporarily *hors de combat*, and who, unable to keep up with the others owing to the pain he was suffering, had now overtaken them.

The first thing this fellow did was to seize a knife which was lying idle, and rush over to me, uttering a savage snarl, his repulsive countenance working hideously with vengeful ferocity. Instinctively I prepared to receive him in the same way as before, whereat he hesitated, and this I believed saved my life, for the others interfered and there was a great hubbub of voices, and a swaying to and fro of the crowd, as more got between him and me. I thought it would have ended in a free fight, but at length the fellow suffered himself to be persuaded, and subsided, growling, by the fire, to make a vehement onslaught upon such meat as still remained.

Having disposed of this he came over to me again. The other Kafirs were for the most part disposing themselves for sleep, while some had lighted pipes, and were puffing away contentedly, conversing in a deep-toned, subdued hum. Indeed, but for my perilous situation the scene was one of wild and vivid picturesqueness—the great overhanging rocks reflecting the glow of the fires or throwing out weird, uncouth silhouettes from moving figures; the red forms of the grouping savages, and the outlandish but not unpleasing tones of their strange tongue; the rolling eyeballs and the gleam of white teeth, as one or other of them opened his mouth in a yawn or a grin.

"What you doing here?" began the fellow.

"I didn't come willingly, I was brought. And now suppose you let me go," I answered.

"Let you go? Ha! See there." And he pointed to something behind me.

I turned. A wide dark space hitherto unnoticed caught my gaze. A black patch it looked like. No, it was a hole, a jagged irregular hole or crevice.

"That hole deep—damn deep," he went on. "Let you go? yes—down there. No find again. We cut your throat first, see—I do that—then throw you in. No find again. Ha!"

I believe I went pale, and I know my flesh crept all over at the prospect of this horrible fate. But I remembered Septimus Matterson's dictum—more than once laid down—with regard to these people: "You must never let them imagine you're afraid of them." So I laughed as I answered—

"You daren't do it. The police would hunt you down, and then the Government would hang every man jack of you."

"Hang? Ha! Not it. We don't care for no damn Government. To-morrow morning you go down hole."

"Why wait till to-morrow?"

The ruffian chuckled.

"See better then. Leave no spoor. Light not good now—might forget something. Body found, perhaps we hang. No body found, then perhaps you not dead. Damn deep that hole. Ha!"

"You'll hang all the same," I said. "You will be spoored here, and there will be plenty of traces of what has become of me."

"No trace. We cut your throat *over* the hole, then throw you in. Now you go to sleep. Morning soon come."

Grinning hideously the fellow rolled his blanket round him and lay down. Most of the others were already asleep, but it was not likely I should follow their example or act upon the ironical suggestion of my tormentor. Was he but trying to frighten me, I tried to think? but then, a word here and there which I had caught, and certain significant glances on the part of my gaolers, seemed to bear out all he had said. They had every motive for getting rid of me, and in such wise as to leave no trace. And here were the means all ready to their hands.

Chapter Sixteen.

A Dash for it.

Now I, Kenrick Holt, who do this tale unfold, am not by nature an especially intrepid animal, wherefore aught in the course of this narrative which might savour of "derring do" had better be set down to impulse, circumstance, or, generically, accident. Further, I have elsewhere undertaken not to spare my own weaknesses, which for present purposes may be taken to mean that the hideous assurance just conveyed to me had left me very badly scared indeed.

In palliation whereof consider the position. In all human certainty the morning light would see me as ruthlessly and as helplessly butchered as the miserable sheep which had just furnished these black cut-throats—and incidentally myself—with an evening meal. A ghastly and horrible fate, in sooth. It might remain shrouded in mystery, even as the ruffian had said, but that was a mere supplementary detail which could be of no subsequent interest to me.

Rescue? That could hardly be. Brian, at any rate, would not desert me. But he could hardly follow up the spoor in the dark; even if he did not credit me with sufficient bushcraft to find my way back to them by some other track, he would never be here in time, and if he was, why, there were twenty or more to one. No, that would be a broken reed to lean upon. Besides, it was more than probable that my late companions would have their own hands full.

The vindictive ruffian who had felt the weight of my foot squatted in front of me, grinning, and every now and then passing a hand across his throat by way of reminder. At last he too grew drowsy, and began to nod. Then he was quickly asleep.

Now I strove to pull myself together, and with an effort rallied my shaken nerves. What was to be done? Not many hours of the night could there be left. Could I free myself? My feet were not bound. Could I not rise and, stepping lightly through the sleeping forms, gain the outside and run for it? But this idea occurred only to be dismissed. Unaided and without the use of my hands I could hardly climb down from the place without meeting with a bad fall in the attempt. If I could but loosen the bonds!

As to this I had been tied up securely, yet not tightly or painfully, consequently felt little or no cramping sensation. Now after a few minutes of careful working I managed to get my right hand free of the lower coil of the thong. But no further could I get it because of a loop, and this held the wrist firmly. I strained and tugged till every muscle and joint seemed cracking, and my brain bursting, but—no yielding. Then I paused to rest, and think out some other plan.

The fire was now a heap of smouldering red ashes, so that the place was almost in darkness, which, though favouring my efforts, was all against me should these meet with success. Then I would want a little light, or was in danger of stumbling over one of the sleepers. Could I once free myself and avoid this, my chances were fair, for Kaffirs are heavy sleepers, and I might gain quite a good start.

But that English-speaking villain seemed possessed with a very demon of unrest, for just then he got up and went over to the fire, trying to blow it into a flame while he spread his black crooked claws over it for warmth. At last he returned to my proximity, and after a good look at me, he lay down again.

All this had taken some while, and it was a good deal longer before I could make even the smallest move; and meanwhile time—precious time—was creeping on. But during it I had been thinking, and thinking hard. In the right hand pocket of my shooting-coat was a knife—a very ordinary pocket-knife—which the rascals must have overlooked in their eagerness to possess themselves of my cartridges. I knew it was there still, for I could feel it. And my right hand, partially freed, could all but reach it.

I tugged and tugged. All to no purpose. The *reim* would not stretch a quarter of an inch further. Then it occurred to me that if I could not get my hand to my pocket, I might still get my pocket to my hand. The ground where I sat was rough and uneven, and by worming myself against a projection of rock I found I could do something in that direction. It was tedious work—tedious and difficult. Twice the knife slipped from my fingers, then at last I grasped it. Grasped it firmly. I was just proceeding to prize it open, when my abominable sentinel moved—stretched himself, snorted, and opened his smoke-filmed eyes. I lay quite still until the brute had subsided again. Then the knife was open.

It was not very sharp, and I had some difficulty in working through the tough raw hide, but none, incidentally, in slicing my fingers over the job; but for this I didn't care. I was now practically free. The coils, cut through in several places, fell apart. Heavens! how the blood surged through my whole being as I realised that escape was within reach. But first of all I had got to make my way over those sleeping forms, and, worst of all, over, that of my restless sentinel.

Now I was ready to make the attempt. Drawing myself cautiously up I gently slid loose from the coil, and as I did so, the abominable ruffian, uttering a muffled exclamation, started up too. But that was all he did. Luckily I had practised a little in the boxing line, and now I let him have it, full, fair and square—a hard, smashing, knock-out blow under the jaw. It was delivered with battering-ram force, and laid him out, flat, inert and absolutely noiseless.

The hammering of my heart, with the exertion and excitement, seemed loud enough to awaken the other sleepers as I stepped, actually *over* some of them. One indeed moved, and I stood ready to administer the same curative to him if he showed sign of waking up, but he subsided again, and most of the others had their blankets over their heads. A moment more, a tense, trying moment, and I stood outside in the open air; and as I did so I noticed the first faint indication of dawn in the far eastern sky.

The declivity was rough and stony, and the faintest clink or dislodgment of a stone might be enough to rouse those within, wherefore it behoved me to tread carefully. But even now, though temporarily free, which way should I turn, for I had but the most rudimentary idea as to my bearings? However, acting on my best judgment, I struck a downward course, and then suddenly a horrible effluvium was wafted to my nostrils.

I was standing upon the brink of a hollow in the heart of the thick bush. The dawn was gradually lightening, and now, looking down into this, I could see that it was thickly strewn with innumerable bones—the bones of oxen and sheep. Two heads, unflayed and decomposed, stared up from the white mass, the great branching horns looking spectral and menacing in the uncertain light. Evidently this was the secret nest of a daring and organised gang of cattle stealers.

While I was debating which way to turn, a sound fell upon my ears which was as the first thrill of security, for it was the unmistakable whicker of a horse. That meant Brian, if not all three of my late companions, returned to search for me. Yet it would not do to make too sure, wherefore as I took my way downward in the direction of the sound I did so in silence, and soon had reason to bless my caution, for after a few minutes of walking there lay before me a small kraal.

It consisted of three huts, whose inmates were probably fast asleep, a thorn enclosure containing a few goats; but, best of all, tied to the gate-post, were two horses. And in these I recognised the horse I had been riding, and one of the stolen ones, by name Punch. To steal down to the spot was the work of very few minutes. Still no sign of life, not even a dog, luckily. Quickly I made my way to the horses. They seemed to recognise me, and whickered again. The goats, too, stampeded to the other side of the kraal. Would the noise waken those villains? Quickly I untied the *reim* which secured my own horse, and twisting a bight of it into his mouth by way of an impromptu bit, I cut through the *reim* that held the other and mounted—of course, barebacked.

Punch at once laid himself out to follow his companion, as I knew he would. But before I had gone a hundred paces I heard another whinny behind. Looking back I beheld two more horses tied to a tree, just beyond the kraal—and even at that distance I recognised Beryl's favourite steed, Meerkat. They had been hidden by a projecting shoulder of bush until now.

Athrill with excitement, for the first time since my capture I began to enjoy the adventure. I would still redeem my pledge, and restore Meerkat, so lost not a moment in turning back to release the other two. But at the same time I saw something else. Following down upon the track of my flight came two or three dark forms, then more and more. My enemies had discovered my escape, and were hot foot in pursuit. I could afford to laugh at them now, well mounted as I was, but—how about Beryl's horse? I should hardly have time to reach it before the savages would be upon me. It was simply a race as to who should get there first.

I have known few excitements in life to equal that moment. The stripe of running, leaping savages converging on my objective, the lithe, ochre-smeared forms flitting through the dark green of the bush, the gleam of assegais—and the closeness of the race. The ground was rough, and riding barebacked as I was, and with only an impromptu bridle, constituted a pretty severe test to my capabilities of horsemanship.

I was there. I leaped off my steed, cut the *reim* which held Meerkat, and twisting it into his mouth in the same way, mounted him—for I was determined to save him, even if all the others had to be sacrificed. Then I cut the *reim* which held the other horse, and with all three following me, I started back, just as the foremost Kafirs leaped from the cover barely thirty yards away.

Mounted as I was, the odds were by no means in my favour, for as I have said the ground was rough and, withal, the bush was thick. And now the whole crowd surged forward, uttering strident hisses and ear-splitting roars, intended to render my steed unmanageable and scatter the others—and indeed how I managed even to stick on, let alone steer through bush and over stones and shuts, I hardly know to this day. Something hit me—something hard and heavy—behind the shoulders, but without effect, the distance being too great. Twenty yards nearer and it would have knocked me headlong, for it was a hard iron-wood kerrie hurled by no unpractised hand, and as I pressed on, the three horses galloping on either side, neighing and capering, but always keeping abreast, the roars and whistles of the pursuing barbarians making the air hideous, I felt that I was in for a very lively time indeed. But the worst of it was that, thanks to the aforesaid roughness of the ground, they could travel nearly as fast as I could, and more than once I looked over my shoulder with something like despair as I saw how untiringly and persistently they kept up the pursuit. At this rate my mount would soon get blown, nor was I sure I was taking the right direction.

We were racing up a long stony slope, rather more clear of bush than hitherto. Poor Meerkat was not in hard condition, and I was beginning to regret not having stuck to my first mount. Then the bang of a gun away on my left front scattered all reflections to the winds.

"This way, Holt! This way!" sang out a voice, and at the same time bang went another shot.

As I proceeded to follow out Brian's injunction I looked round, just in time to see a spurt of dust fly up very near in front of my pursuers, where the bullet had struck. These had halted, and as just then there was another bang, and another bullet fell rather nearer than the first, they evidently concluded it was too warm, and began to drop down into cover.

Brian was lying comfortably ensconced in a bush, inserting a fresh cartridge. "I only shot to scare," he said, in his cool way, as I came up. "They'll stop now."

"Are you all alone?"

"Yes. Came back to look after you."

"And jolly near too late you were, old chap, for if I hadn't managed to slip my own cable, I'd have been lying at the bottom of an infernal hole at this moment, with my throat cut from ear to ear. That's what was sticking out for me at daybreak."

"So? Did you know those chaps were stalking you down when you started back for the two remaining horses?" he said.

"Rather. I raced them for it. You see, I promised to bring back Meerkat, and I'd got to do it. But—did you see that part of it?"

"*Ja*. Watched you all the time, but concluded that this was the best place to effect a diversion in your favour. Well, Holt—you won't mind my saying so—but you're no fool of an imported Britisher, and that's a dead cert. I don't expect Trask would have come out of things in that way."

"Oh, yes he would," I answered with cheerful magnanimity, for I was in secret hugely pleased with myself—not from any innate vanity, but because I should return to Gonya's Kloof with enhanced prestige. And for certain reasons I could do with all the prestige I could capture, just then.

We had fallen back on where Brian had left his horse. "You can have my saddle as soon as we can get out of these kloofs," he said. "I expect you'll get sick of riding barebacked sooner than I shall. At present we needn't lose any time. The other horses? Oh, they'll follow us all right. Later on we can lead them."

"This is a nice, peaceful country of yours, Brian," I said, as we held on our way, for we saw no more of our late enemies. "If this sort of thing happens in time of profound peace, may I ask what it's like in time of war?"

He laughed.

"You may have a chance of seeing for yourself. Well, you have had an adventure, so long"—for I had told him of the sort of night I had spent. "You shouldn't have gone chevying on after those schepsels all by yourself. I kept shouting out to you to come back, and you wouldn't. I thought you'd soon give it up, and we had our own hands pretty full. I started the other two off with the oxen, and came back to look for you. Thought I'd find you'd only been spending the night under a bush."

Chapter Seventeen.

"Hand to the Labour—Heart and Hand."

"Bring back Meerkat," had been Beryl's parting injunction, and I had fulfilled it to the letter. And as I restored her favourite horse, literally with my own hands—and none the worse for his enforced travels, though the other two returned with sore backs—I was conceited enough to think that the pleased light of welcome that came over Beryl's sweet face was not entirely due to satisfaction at his recovery, and that approbation of his rescuer bore some small share therein.

"Well done, Kenrick," sang out Iris, clapping her hands. "Man, but you're no sort of a raw Britisher anyhow." And I own that the dear child's frank and homely form of approval fell gratefully upon my ears just then.

"You should have seen Revell sabreing them all right and left with a sjambok when they cheeked him at that kraal," guffawed Trask. "Oh—h—"

The last in a subdued howl, evolved by the contact of Brian's boot with the speaker's shin, under the table. For in another moment Trask would have blundered out the whole story as a joke of the first water, in anticipation whereof Revell was beginning to redden furiously.

"He got us out of that in the nick of time," struck in Brian with his wonted tact. "Pass on the grog, Trask. Help yourself first—thanks. Well, we've brought back the whole plunder, except one of the oxen, and Kenrick's gun. The first they've scoffed, and the second we shan't see again, I'm afraid. Eh, dad?"

"I'm afraid not. You've done well—very well. I never expected you'd recover so much. I'm very much obliged to you fellows for your help."

Of course we all disclaimed any expression of thanks; but later on what does this prince of good fellows do but send for a first-rate gun to replace my missing piece. No, he would not listen to any protest. I had lost my own in recovering his property, therefore it was only fair he should make it good.

Later on, too, when Beryl heard the story of my own perilous and nerve-trying experience—(much of the detail of our expedition had, for obvious reasons, been kept from the children)—she said—

"Why did you do it? Why did you run such a terrible risk? I would sooner have lost all the horses in the world. Heavens! and you were so near being murdered! No, you ought not to have taken such a risk. Why, I should never have forgiven myself—never. It is too horrible."

She was intensely moved. Her eyes softened strangely, and there was something of a quaver in her voice. And yet my first impressions had credited Beryl Matterson with a cold disposition! Had we been alone together now I don't know what I might have said or done—or rather I believe I do know. As it was, I answered lightly—

"Oh, I don't suppose it would have come to that. Probably they were only trying to scare me, and, by Jove! they succeeded, I'll own to that. When it came to the point they'd likely have turned me adrift. Don't you think so, Mr Matterson?"

"No, I don't. They'd have killed you as sure as eggs," was the decisive reply. "They're a mighty *schelm* lot up Kameel Kloof way, and there has been more than one disappearance of white men during the last few years. But you can't bring them to book. They swarm like red ants in that location, and no Kafir will ever give another away."

In point of fact I was not ill-pleased with this decision, simply and solely because the peril I had come through would enhance my interest in the eyes of Beryl, especially as it had been incurred in her particular service.

Our return had been effected without incident or opposition, and to me there was a strong smack of the old border raiding kind of business as we brought back the recovered spoil, recovered by our own promptitude and dash. As for myself, I had undergone some experience of the noble savage in his own haunts, and began to feel quite a seasoned frontiersman. And yet barely three months ago I had been worrying along in the most approved mill-horse round in a City office. Heavens! what a change had come into my life.

Immediately on our return, all concerned in it had held a council of war, confined rigidly to the four of us. The fewer in the know the better, Brian had declared, wherefore he had not disclosed the whole facts of the case even to his father. One of the thieves had been shot, whether killed or disabled of course we had no idea. On that we must keep our own counsel, absolutely and strictly, and to make assurance doubly sure we must never so much as mention the matter again even among ourselves.

Incidentally the rest of us thought it just as well that Trask had accounted for him, because Trask was the weak link in the chain, whereas now that he was the one most concerned, self-preservation alone would keep him from giving away the affair under an impulse of senseless brag.

"You see," pronounced Brian, "as long as we keep dark the Kafirs'll keep dark, too. They'll think nothing of one fellow getting hurt, because it's quite in accordance with their laws and customs that some one should get hurt in a little affair of the kind. But if we start stirring up things—setting the police on to the track, and so forth—why then it's likely the other business will crop up, and that'll be more than awkward, for the *schelm* wasn't even going for us, but running away. Running away, mind. There's no doubt about it but that we—or rather, Holt—struck upon a regular nest of cattle-thieves; but we can do nothing further under the circumstances, nothing whatever. So mum's the word, absolutely. Is that understood?"

All hands agreed to this, but none more emphatically than Trask, who, by the way, was a little less proud of his feat now that it was put in this new and exceedingly awkward light.

"Very well, then, that's settled," declared Brian, characteristically dismissing the affair from his mind.

After this things settled down at Gonya's Kloof, ordinarily and without incident. And yet, to me, so radical was the change compared with all my former life, that every day seemed replete with incident, even what to the others was mere ordinary routine. I threw myself with zest into everything, and both Brian and his father declared after a month or two that if I went on at this rate I should know as much as they could teach me before I had been with them a year, and already knew a great deal more than Trask did after four: a pronouncement which was exceedingly gratifying to me.

I look back upon those days as among the very happiest of my life. Not that it was all picnicking by any means. There was plenty of work—hard, at times distasteful, even unpleasant. There were times when such meant rising in the dark, saddling up in the grey dawn, and spending the whole long day ranging the veldt in quest of strayed stock, and that beneath a steady, cold, incessant downpour, which soon defied mere waterproof, and would have extinguished the comforting pipe but for the over-sheltering hat brim. Or, substitute for the downpour a fierce sun, burning down upon hill and kloof, until one felt almost light-headed with the heat. Or the shearing, which meant a daily round from dawn till dark in a hot stuffy shed, redolent of grease and wool, and sheep, and musky, perspiring natives—and this running into weeks. But there was always something, and seldom indeed could one call any time actually and indisputably one's own.

Does this sound hardly compatible with the statement I have made above? It need not; for however hard or arduous the work, I was happy in it. I felt that I was mastering the secret of a new walk in life, and to me a highly attractive and independent one. I was simply glowing with health, and in condition as hard as nails, for although the weather would now and again run into a trying extreme, on the whole the climate was gloriously healthy and exhilarating. Then, too, I was sharing in the only real home I had ever known—certainly the very happiest one I had ever seen. It mattered not how hard the day had been, there was always the evening, and we would sit restfully out on the stoep, smoking our pipes and chatting beneath the dark firmament aflame with stars, while the shrill bay of jackals ran weirdly along the distant hillside, and the ghostly whistle of plover circled dimly overhead and around, and the breaths of the night air were sweet with the distillation from flowering plant or shrub. Or, within the house Beryl would play for us, or sing a song or two in her sweet, natural, unaffected way. Or even the harmless squabbling of the two children would afford many a laugh.

"Tired, Kenrick?" said Septimus Matterson one such evening, after an unusually hard day of it. "Ha-ha! Stock-farming isn't all picnicking and sport, is it?"

"Not much; but then I never expected it would be," I answered. "I am only just healthily tired—just enough to thoroughly appreciate this prize comfortable chair."

"Anyway, you're looking just twice the man you were when you came. Isn't he, Beryl?"

"Hardly that, father, or we should have to widen the front door," she answered demurely. We all laughed.

"Man, Beryl. That reminds me of Trask, when he tries to be funny," grunted that impudent pup, George.

"That reminds *me* that it's high time you were in bed, George," returned Beryl, equable and smiling. "So off you go there now, and sharp."

Her word was law in matters of this kind, admitting of no appeal, so Master George slouched off accordingly, making a virtue of necessity by declaring he was beastly tired, and further had only stopped up to help amuse us; which final speech certainly carried that effect.

Beryl remained talking with us a little while longer, then she, too, went inside.

"What on earth I should do without my girl, Kenrick, I don't know," thereafter said her father. "Yet I suppose I shall have to some day."

"Will you?" I said vacuously, for the words raised an uncomfortable twinge.

"Why, yes, I suppose so, in the ordinary way of things."

"Oh! um—yes, ah! I suppose so," I echoed idiotically, feeling devoutly thankful that the gloom of night concealed a stupid reddening which I could feel spreading over my asinine countenance, and wondering if the other detected the inconsequent inanity of the rejoinder begotten of an *arrière-pensée*. But I realised keenly the only side of the situation that would reconcile me to Beryl's father having to do without her.

I had now had time to straighten out my affairs in England; and arrange for having my capital transferred to this country, though this could not be done yet, by reason of its investment requiring notice of withdrawal. I had caused such of my personal belongings as I needed—and such were not extensive— to be shipped out to me, also some money which I could touch, and this I promptly invested in live stock, under the advice of my most competent of instructors. So by now I reckoned myself fairly and squarely launched. By the way, the man whose boat had constituted the first step in my change of fortunes, having found out my identity, had put in a claim for compensation, but had been directed to wait. Now he too was paid in full, and so everybody was satisfied.

We were nearing midsummer, i.e. Christmas and the New Year, but the intensifying heat notwithstanding, the face of the veldt was smiling and green, for we had had a series of splendid rains. Such a season, it was pronounced, had not been known for years. Stock was fat and thriving, and there was little or no disease. Even our turbulent neighbours had quieted down, and were busy ploughing and sowing, with the result that there was an abnormal but welcome lull in cattle lifting and other maraudings along the border, whose white inhabitants were, for the nonce, content.

"It's Kenrick who has brought us luck," declared Iris, with a decisive nod of her pretty head, as we were metaphorically rubbing our hands over the existing state of things. "I've read somewhere that it's always lucky to pick up a waif and stray."

We shouted at this. Then Brian said—

"I rather think it was the waif and stray who picked you up, *kleintje*! What price swimming too far out, and the sharks, eh?"

"*Nouw ja*, that's true," she conceded. "But you see, he was bringing us luck even then. You couldn't get on without me," concluded Miss Impudence. Whereat we shouted again.

Chapter Eighteen.

Developments.

"Well, who's for church to-day?" said Brian, one fine Sunday morning as we straggled in to breakfast. "There's one, anyhow," he appended, as Beryl appeared, clad in a riding habit. "Wouldn't you rather drive, Beryl? It's going to be hot."

"No. I think I'll ride," she answered, busying herself with the cups and saucers. "Meerkat wants some exercise, he's getting too lively even for me. Are you up to going, dad?"

"Make it rather a heavy load, won't it? Still, George might ride. That'll make three of us—quite enough load too, for that heavy cart."

This was a suggestion which, overtly on the part of one of its hearers, privily on that of another, met with scant approval. On that of George because he preferred being driven, and the shade of the cart tilt, and a comfortable seat, to the trouble of jogging over ten miles of road in the sun, and on a possibly rough-going mount. On that of myself because I did not in the least want George on this occasion, nor anybody else. I wanted the ride alone with Beryl. In fact, I had more than half set up this arrangement when we had heard the day before that there would be church service at Stacey's farm at the distance above stated, whither a parson had unexpectedly turned up.

"Well, I don't think I shall go at all," went on the last speaker. "I don't feel much up to it."

"You're very wicked, dad," chipped in Iris, with a shake of the head. "Why, it's six weeks since last church Sunday."

"Quite right, kitten," laughed her father, reaching out a hand to stroke her bright sunny hair. "Never mind. You can behave twice as well as usual because I'm not there."

"Well, I'll stay with you."

"No, no. I can't allow that," he laughed. "Not for a moment."

In point of fact, the proposal had required some self-denial, for these occasions were highly popular with the children by reason of the outing involved, and the gathering at the other end, wherefore Miss Iris suffered herself to be over-ruled quite placidly. The said gatherings were of irregular occurrence; this scattered flock for that very reason being but little shepherded.

Septimus Matterson hardly ever talked about religion or its principles; he went one better—he practised them. For the young ones that sort of training was Beryl's province, he reckoned; while as for Brian and myself, why, we were old enough to know our own minds in such matters and act accordingly. If we chose to attend the somewhat irregular ministrations at Stacey's we could do so; if not, that was our own business.

To-day, especially, I very much did so choose. It was one of those heavenly mornings in late autumn which I don't believe you can get outside South Africa—no, not even in Italy—for where else will you find a sky so deeply, so vividly blue; such a sunlight sweep of gold upon rolling seas of green foliage; or open grass veldt studded with delicate-fronded mimosa; such an atmosphere too, which, with no sharp touch in it, is warm and yet exhilarating at the same time. And the unending vistas opened up—the rise of hills, near and far, green-crested, or stately with a crown of bronze-faced cliff, glowing red gold in the generous sunlight; against a background of ever-vivid unbroken blue. Small wonder that on such a day, as Beryl and I cantered along, our spirits were at the highest.

"I don't ride Meerkat half enough," she said. "Look how lively he is."

I did look, and the picture was worth it. The horse, holding high his stag-like head, deep-shouldered, delicate-limbed, yet full of fire and muscle, hardly restrainable in his sportive freshness, would have taken a good many women all they knew to manage. Yet this one sat him to perfection, firm, light in the saddle, swaying with his every movement as though for the time being part of the steed himself; graceful, smiling, snowing no sign of heat or effort, just a little glow of health and contentment flushing her cheeks. No, Beryl never looked better than on her favourite horse. To-day she looked splendid.

I had arranged this ride along with her for a purpose, and the readiness wherewith she had concurred in the arrangement might have meant nothing, but I preferred to think the contrary—that she understood my purpose and concurred in it. I had been here now some months, and we had seen each other daily, and the complete cordiality of our intercourse, with never a hitch, never a jar, so far from waning, had, if possible, increased. I had resolved to-day to bring matters to a head; yet in the—to me—complete happiness of this our ride together, I seemed to defer anything that might break the charm. I would leave it to our return ride. So we chatted on as usual, and gaily, about one thing and another, and then, even if I had wished it otherwise it was too late, for we could see the white tilts of Cape carts and buggies coming from different directions along road and veldt path—riders, too, like ourselves, but all converging upon the common objective. Then the increasing "whang-whang" of a bell, as we drew nearer to this, seemed to cause a general hurry up on the part of all within sight.

I off-saddled our horses and knee-haltered them, among others performing the same operation; Beryl the while having gone forward to greet the people of the place and other acquaintances, and these were many, for of course everybody knew everybody. Just as we were going in Trask bore down upon us.

"I say, Miss Matterson, and you, Holt. Come in front, will you, and help to make a choir. I'm rounding up as many as I can."

"Not going to have Christmas over again, eh, Trask?" I said maliciously, the point of which being that Trask, who really did know something about music, and was *ex officio* organist, or to be more accurate, harmoniumist, had on the occasion referred to undertaken to launch out into anthems and carols and all sorts of things unknown to the multitude: such ambitious soarings, and the letting off of wholly extemporised and weird harmonic fireworks on the instrument, which he called "accompaniment" resulting in the silence, by relays, of the whole body of singers; though not before the latter had ingeniously if unconsciously blended the "Adeste fideles," the "Old Hundredth," "Coming through the Rye," and other historic and popular melodies into one inspiring whole. It may be readily imagined that of this fiasco Trask did not quickly hear the end, wherefore he liked not my present reference.

"Oh, go to blazes, Holt," he retorted pepperily. "I'd like to know what you'd have done in my place with such a lot of—of—" and here he was obliged to stop short, remembering that Beryl had been one of the offenders. She, catching my eye, was thoroughly enjoying the situation.

"All right, Mr Trask," she answered. "We'll do what we can. Only you mustn't try and make us do what we can't."

The little plain, whitewashed building—which Stacey had erected on his farm, and was inordinately proud of, and fond of alluding to as "my church"—was nearly full, a thoroughly representative congregation of stock farmers, and their families. Many, like ourselves, had ridden over, and there was a sprinkling of habits among the feminine section of the gathering, eke a proportion of pretty faces. But, great Hercules! there was nothing here to come near Beryl. Looking round, I realised with a glow of pride that, compared with these, she was as a lily among daisies and—she was with me, standing by me, sitting by me, kneeling by me. It seemed—or I wanted it to seem—as though I had a kind of proprietary interest in her.

Frankly, I own to not being much of a church-goer; far indeed be it from me to cast a slight on those who are. It is sad, though a fact, but the process— especially in the morning—has a soporific effect. Yet here, in this little whitewashed building, with the blue sky glimpsed through the open windows, the hum of bees and the strange call of birds in the bush without, wafting in to mingle with the parson's voice and the murmurs of the congregation, I did not feel drowsy in the least. The graceful habit-clad figure beside me, the profile at which I stole more than one side glance, the sweet true voice, the mere delight of listening to which constituted, I fear, the sole assistance on my part towards Trask's choral aspirations—there was no room for boredom or drowsiness in such proximity; and if this be objected to as a substituting of the creature for the Creator, well, still in my blundering untheological mind I have an idea, which I couldn't express intelligibly to save my life, that on this occasion the influence was something more than a mere earthly one. But let that pass.

After the service we streamed out into the sunlight, and tongues began to wag on all sides.

"Do persuade your brother to stay and have dinner with us, Miss Matterson," said a voice on the other side of Beryl. "We can't; and it's much too long for poor little Iris to wait if he persists in taking her back at once. Of course you'll stay—and Mr Holt."

The speaker was one of the two girls who had made their appearance what time I had got Iris out of the sea at East London, and we had often laughed over it together, and the figure I must have cut. Then old Stacey came up and seconded the invite so heartily that Beryl gave way. But Brian was as adamant. He wanted to get back, for several reasons, he said. Beryl and I knew more than one of them at any rate. As a matter of fact, Brian was a bit of a misogynist. He detested fooling around among a pack of women, he used to say; and the Stacey girls he held in particular aversion, which was ungrateful of him, as they happened to cherish a scarcely disguised admiration for his unappreciative self. So George and poor little Iris were carried summarily off, greatly to the disgust of the latter.

We who remained made ourselves festive enough. Old Stacey, though somewhat shaky over his aspirates, was not half a bad old sort, and the girls showed to far the best advantage in their own home. They made themselves exceedingly pleasant to Beryl and myself, and if they had a way of bracketing us together, so to say, it was by no means displeasing to me, for I had got into a way myself of feeling a sort of proprietary right in her, when we were among other people. If she noticed this, assuredly she could not have resented it; at times I would even let myself think she unconsciously reciprocated it. She would often refer to me upon some debated matter, for instance, as if mine was the opinion which rendered it final.

We took leave of our entertainers a couple of hours before sundown, in great good humour with ourselves and all the world. A misgiving had at one time seized me lest Trask should inflict himself upon us, as at any rate part of our way lay together, but he had taken himself off much earlier—and now we were alone. Not a soul was in sight, not even a house. The undulation of the veldt, green and gold in the westering sun, stretching away on either side, was as if deserted by man. Not by animate Nature, though. A troop of monkeys skipped across our path, momentarily scaring our horses, and chattering at us from the tree-tops; and bird voices were never still. Several blue cranes were shambling along just off our way, and the incessant cooing of doves, near and far, blended melodiously with the fair and peaceful evening scene.

Yes, the happiness and peace of the day were upon me, as if this fair scene were an earnest of the happiness and peace which had filled my life of late. Was it a reflection of that which should continue to irradiate it? Alas and alas, could I but have foreseen! Yet what misgiving could strike me then, what foreboding that this day was the last—the very last day of happiness or peace for me, and indeed for others, for a long time to come?

"Well, Kenrick, and what is the subject of that very deep meditation?"
I started. I had forgotten how long I had been plunged in silence.
"You are," I said.
"Me?"
Her eyes opened wide. There was the most delightfully alluring little smile, half demure, half mischievous, playing around her lips. Then, as I took in her whole sweet personality, as I looked at her and thought how the next few moments were to decide whether that sweet and gracious personality were to belong to me for the remainder of our lives, or not—my pulses were bounding and beating at such a rate that I wondered how I should get out even two consecutive and coherent words. Yet it must be done, now and here.
"Listen, Beryl," I began. "There is something I want you to hear, and that you must hear. I—"

"Hullo! Hi, you good people! Hold on a bit and give us a chance to come up."

And that infernal Trask came clattering upon our heels, having spotted us from the road which led from his place. Well, there was an end of everything. My opportunity was gone—for that day, at any rate; and I hold a superstition to the effect that opportunities have a way of not recurring.

"Thought I'd ride over and make an evening of it at your place, Miss Matterson," he rattled on. "A man gets a bit hipped sometimes all by himself, you know. So glad I fell in with you like this."

Beryl answered sweetly that so were we, and that they were always glad to see him, and so forth. While I—well, at that moment I could cheerfully have murdered Trask with my own hand.

Chapter Nineteen.

Concerning a Tragedy.

A shot rang out, faint and distant, upon the slumbrous morning air.

"There's that young *schelm* George at work," remarked Brian, raising himself on one elbow to listen.

"At play, rather," I laughed.

"That's it. He's a jolly sight too fond of cutting school in favour of a buck-hunt. The governor spoils him far too much. I wouldn't."

George's education at that time was effected through the agency of a farm-school about seven miles off, whither he rode over five days per week; in theory at least, for few indeed were the weeks out of which he did not contrive to filch one extra day—not to help us in any work, oh dear no, for he looked upon it as a distinct grievance to be required to do any such thing—but to amuse himself. To-day he had started for the Zwaart Kloof alone to try and sneak a bush-buck. But if the young rascal was at play, Brian and I were tolerably hard at work; had been rather, for we had spent the morning strengthening and repairing the bush fence of one of our enclosures; and chopping mimosa boughs and then beating them into place is a fairly muscular phase of manual labour on a hot day. Now we were pausing for a rest.

But if it was a hot day it was a lovely one—lovely and cloudless. A shimmer of heat lay upon the wide valley, and all the life of the veldt was astir—bird voices calling far and near, the melodious hoot of the hoepoe from the distance, the quaint, half-whistling, half-rasping dialogue of a pair of yellow thrushes hard by, or the bold cheery pipe of sheeny-winged spreuws flashing among the bush sprays. Insect sounds, too; the bass boom of some big beetle rising above the murmuring hum of bees, and the screech of innumerable crickets. In sooth, if our work was hard, it was set amid exquisite surroundings, and, as though no element of romance should be lacking, I thought to discern from time to time the flutter of a light dress about the homestead, nearly a mile distant beneath us, as though reminding myself, at any rate, that after labour came recreation, which to me spelt Beryl.

No opportunity had I found for renewing the subject so ruthlessly interrupted yesterday during our ride home, and now I was tormented by an uncomfortable misgiving as to whether Beryl was not purposely avoiding any such opportunity.

We got up from the grateful shade under which we had been resting, and, hatchet in hand, started in on another spell, and for nearly an hour were chopping and hauling, and banging the great mimosa boughs into place so that the thorns should interlace with those already laid down. Then Brian suggested we should go back to dinner, and return and finish up when it was cooler, but before we could put this plan into execution the trampling of hoofs was heard drawing rapidly near, at a pace that was out of the way reckless and unnecessary.

"That's George," said Brian, "but if he's shot anything he hasn't loaded it up. Hey! Hullo! What luck, George?"

The latter would have passed without seeing us. Now as he reined in and approached us we saw that the boy's face was as white as death, and his eyes staring with the most awful look of horror and fear.

"Man, what's wrong?" said Brian sharply, his own bronzed countenance turning a kind of whitey-brown. "Not shot yourself, have you?"

"No, not myself—not myself," the boy managed to jerk out. And then he broke into a wild fit of sobbing.

Brian's face grew still whiter.

"Is it somebody else, then? But you went out alone."

"Yes—I—I—I w-went out alone."

"George, pull yourself together, man. Whatever's happened; we're losing time. Don't be an ass now. Tell us all about it."

This he managed to do; and a woeful and dismaying tale it was that he spasmodically unfolded. Reft of its incoherencies—natural under the circumstances—this was the sum of it.

He had reached the Zwaart Kloof, and having left his horse was stealthily advancing to peer over the brink of a small krantz, beneath which a bush-buck was sometimes lying. This time, instead of a bush-buck there were a lot of Kafir boys larking about the kloof. He told them to clear out, but, seeing he couldn't get at them immediately, they were cheeky and laughed at him. So he pointed his gun at them, calling out that he'd shoot the whole lot if they didn't clear—intending, of course, only to frighten them—and then—how it happened he could not for the life of him tell—but the gun went off, the heavy charge of treble A simply raking the group. Two were killed outright, for they never moved, and two more lay wounded and screaming. The rest ran away, and he himself, reckoning that the best plan was to get help as soon as possible, had started for home as fast as his horse could carry him.

Such was the miserable story which the wretched boy managed to unfold, and meanwhile we were walking rapidly towards the house.

"Oh, I never meant to do anything but scare them, Brian—I swear before God I didn't!" sobbed the poor little chap, in an agony of remorse.

"Of course you didn't, George. We all know that. Here, give me the gun."

"Take it—take it. I never want to touch a gun again in my life. Oh, what is to be done? What will the dad say?"

Septimus Matterson did not "say" much, but the expression of his face was as that of a man undergoing acute physical pain. Meanwhile Brian had been thinking out a plan, which was to proceed at once to the spot with two of the farm Kafirs, and see what could be done for the wounded boys. Beryl volunteered to accompany him, but this he vetoed with his wonted decisiveness.

"On no account, Beryl. You stay here—you'll be far more useful that way. Now turn me out some bandages, and a flask of brandy."

This was done in a moment, and he was ready to start.

"No, no, Kenrick," he said, as I announced my intention of accompanying him. "You must stay here too. Don't move from the house either. Do you hear? It's hard to say what may happen, and you'll be wanted. There's no telling what trouble this affair may stir up. You understand?"

Then I did understand. The ominous significance of his tone sufficed for that. But all attempts to convince him that his place lay here too, were futile.

"Those who ran away will have obtained help from their own people by now," I urged. But in vain.

The while Beryl was striving to reassure her young brother, and she had all her work cut out for her, for the poor boy's remorse was dreadful to witness, and to do him justice no thought of potential pains and penalties hanging over his own head entered into this, which was actuated by sheer horror of having taken life—several lives, for all we could at present tell.

"It was pure accident, George, we all know that," she said. "And you must do all you can in reparation. You will remember that, dear, won't you, whatever happens."

"Oh, they can hang me if they like. The sooner the better."

"They won't do that, at any rate. It was an accident." And then Beryl went on to soothe and comfort the poor boy, and the sweet magnetism of her voice and words bore good effect.

This and more I overheard while discussing the situation with their father.

"This is a most awful and deplorable thing to have happened, Kenrick," the latter was saying. "As soon as Brian comes back, and we know the extent of the damage, I shall have to send into Fort Lamport and notify the Resident Magistrate. The boy may even be sent for trial for manslaughter."

"But the thing was a sheer accident. Surely they won't hold a kid like that criminally responsible."

"There's no knowing what Shattuck'll do or won't do—he's such an officious fool."

"Yes, he's all that," I agreed, having an acid recollection of the demeanour of the official in question over such a trivial matter as signing a firearm permit.

"He has a 'down' on us farmers too, and will always favour a Kafir under the Masters and Servants Act if he gets a chance. It's just the same in stock stealing cases. They ought to have put him into some Western Province magistracy. A man like that has no business on the frontier."

"I blame myself mostly," went on the speaker. "I ought never to have allowed a young feather-head like George to go out alone with a gun. The only thing is, I have always believed in boys learning to shoot as soon as possible in a country like this. Even girls ought to. Beryl can."

"Rather," I said. "Haven't I seen evidence of that?"

Septimus Matterson was looking worn and ill, and very anxious. He had been ailing for some days past, and this deplorable eventuality had not exactly gone towards setting him up. I remembered Beryl's remark about her father's life not being a "good" one, from an insurance point of view, and felt more than anxious on his behalf.

"You are not looking at all well yourself," I said. "Now, don't let this affair get on your mind too much. It'll all blow over, depend upon it."

"Oh, I'm all right, Kenrick. Don't you worry about me. I suppose Beryl has been filling you up with some of her coddling notions. She wants to coddle me, the dear girl—always telling me to take care of myself; and so on. I pretend to take it all in, of course. Hallo! Wait a minute—" he broke off.

He went outside, returning directly with a field-glass.

"Quite a lot of them," he said, handing it to me after a look down the kloof. "We shall have trouble over this, Kenrick, apart from any cussedness Shattuck may spring on us. I wish Brian was back again."

So did I, as I stood with the glass to my eyes. For a number of Kafirs were coming up the kloof, some mounted but most on foot—the latter coming along at a swinging trot to keep pace with the horsemen. And that there might be no doubt as to their hostile intent, I could see that all carried a couple of business-like kerries apiece, and not a few of them assegais as well.

"Hadn't we better arm ourselves and barricade the house?" I suggested.

"No, no. We mustn't seem afraid of them. Still, there's no harm in dropping a revolver into our right hand pockets, in case of accidents. We'll talk to them here."

We went inside and quickly loaded a revolver apiece. At a word from her father Beryl got down her own pistol, loaded it, and tranquilly pocketed it. Poor little Iris was looking very scared, but was quite quiet.

"Keep these children entirely out of sight, Beryl," enjoined her father, "and it'll be no harm if you don't show yourself during the *indaba*. There may be a lot of bluster and talking big; but it won't come to anything worse, so don't be scared, any of you."

"I wish Brian were here, father," said Beryl anxiously.

"So do I, but he isn't. And if ever you've known of a situation in which Brian has proved unable to take care of himself, I haven't. He'll be all right."

The dogs, which had been walking up and down outside, growling, now broke into such a clamour as to drown all speech, and charged furiously down upon the advancing Kafirs as the foremost came in sight round the bend of the cattle kraal, and would hardly be called off, even by their master's most imperative tones, aided by two or three kerries shied at them by the newcomers, an act in itself significant of the ugly and dangerous mood which was upon our unwelcome visitors.

"Seems as if we'd got the whole of Kuliso's location," said Septimus Matterson, as we took in the crowd which was advancing upon us. The kloof indeed seemed black with Kafirs. Those who had horses dismounted as they came in sight of the house, and the whole body of them came straight on with a fellness of purpose that augured the worst.

It was a tense moment. Our unpleasantness with the people at the kraal on our way in pursuit of the stolen oxen was nothing to this for a situation. There must have been hundreds and hundreds of Kafirs here; hulking, ochre-smeared barbarians, some of gigantic stature, all with an expression of menace and determination and ferocity upon their savage faces. Others, too, were coming on in the distance to swell their numbers. My hand was closed round the butt of the revolver in my pocket. I looked at Septimus Matterson. He had not moved, and was still standing, calm and undismayed, confronting the furious and threatening rout.

Chapter Twenty.

A Fell Alternative.

"Halt!"

Septimus Matterson put forth his hand and uttered just the one word, and the effect was like fire applied to the train. A roar of menace and fury ran through the whole crowd. A forest of dark grisly hands seemed to tighten with murderous grip upon kerries, and assegais were shaken at us; but the injunction was obeyed. The foremost were about fifty paces from us, and others came swarming up in the background, forming an immense half circle.

"We have come for the boy. He must die. He has slain two of our sons—and they are of the House of Kuliso. He must die."

Such was the promising manner in which negotiations were opened. Now I had been studying the Xosa tongue rather diligently since I had been at Gonya's Kloof, and had acquired quite a smattering of it. Septimus Matterson, of course, spoke it perfectly.

"Were they of the house of the chief?" he said. "But where is Kuliso?"

"Bring out the boy," they roared in response. "He must die. He has taken two lives, and he must die twice. Bring him out, *Umlúngu*, or it will be the worse for all of you."

"Hear now, *amadoda*" came the reply, "the thing was an accident, entirely an accident, and for it I will make due and complete compensation according to your custom. Retire now and carry my word to Kuliso and his *amapakati*, for surely I see no man of any note here."

This was indeed the case, and augured the worst. The wily chiefs could plead afterwards that any outrage that might occur was the work of an irresponsible mob. The latter, in no wise pacified, broke forth again.

"Compensation? Not so. Blood for blood. A life for a life—or rather for two lives. That is the word of the people. And the two lives were of the house of the chief. Bring out the boy. Bring him out."

The wild hubbub of voices grew louder and louder, and the ferocious crowd closed in upon us nearer and nearer. Sticks were brandished, and I could see more than one ruffian handling his assegai all ready for a cast. It was a fearful moment. Our lives seemed to hang upon a hair—and worse, for were we struck down or assegaied, would these barbarians, in the fury of their blood lust, spare one living being within that house?

"Shall we get inside and shoot?" I said hurriedly and in a low tone, without turning my face from the enemy.

"No. We'd do no good that way. The bluster may wear itself out."

"Attend, *Umlúngu*," called out one great voice. "If the boy is not handed over to us immediately, we will take him. But first of all we will kill all here."

"You will have to do that first, Sibuko," was the stern reply, "and in doing it many of yourselves will die."

Sibuko! I remembered the name, and now, looking at its wearer, I remembered him. It was the big Kafir to whom Brian had administered a well-deserved thrashing on the morning after my arrival, and now this ruffian was the leading spirit of the whole ferocious crew. We were indeed in a bad way. It was manifest that no white man could surrender his son into the power of these savages, even apart from their curiously significant promise that he should die "twice." But—the way out?

"This is what shall be done," went on Matterson. "The boy shall be sent into the town to be tried by the magistrate. The laws of the Government are there, and are for all. Kuliso cannot make his own laws, unless the Amandhlambe are prepared to make war upon the Government. When a white man kills another he is tried and punished for it. When a Kafir kills another the same happens. Both are punished by the same laws, the laws of the Government."

I thought I observed a tendency among them to cool down at these words, but that ruffian Sibuko walked up and down, haranguing them and flourishing his kerrie, and in the result a number of them went round to the back of the house. Well, this did not distress us much. We thought that Beryl would know what to do in such an emergency.

"The boy!" they howled again. "Give him up to us, or we will kill you all and roast you in the flames of your burning house. Now, *Umlúngu*, bring out the boy."

Septimus Matterson put up his hand. The clamour stilled.

"Listen," he said, and his voice rang out loud and clear. "You shall not have the boy. We hold twelve lives here," drawing his revolver and pointing it, an example I promptly followed. "Before you kill us twelve men shall die. You know me."

The silence that followed upon the tumult was well-nigh alarming. The clamourous savages had imagined that they had two unarmed men to deal with, and now the sight of two business-like six-shooters pointed straight at them seemed to throw a different light on affairs. They were hundreds, it was true. But that twelve men, or near it, would certainly fall before they could reach us they fully realised, the point of which was that none of them wanted to constitute one of the twelve. I stole a sidelong look at Septimus Matterson, and thought to discover something of what had daunted them, for his face wore the aspect of the strong, quiet man thoroughly roused, and, more dangerous still, deadly cool through it all. At the same time came Beryl's voice from the other side of the house, sharp and clear upon the silence, saying in their tongue—

"These two guns are heavily loaded with buckshot. I will pour all four barrels into the mass of you if you make a step forward. After that I still hold six lives."

Looking back, I can hardly ever have gone through a more strained crisis of tense excitement than that moment afforded. The great crescent of ochre-smeared, infuriated savages seemed to shrink into itself, as though concentrating for a decisive rush, and indeed I don't care to think what the next moment might have brought forth had not a diversion occurred.

Coming up the kloof at a swift canter were four mounted figures. Police? No. Three of them were Kafirs, the fourth a white man.

"*Au*! *Namhlanje*!" went up from the crowd, and heads were turned to watch the new arrivals.

Now "Namhlanje" was Brian's native name, which, meaning "to-day," had been bestowed upon him as characterising his quick decisive way of doing things, and when linked with it was uttered another name, Usivulele, I began to think the crisis was past, for the name was that of one of the Ndhlambe chiefs, whose influence was hardly inferior to that of Kuliso himself.

Hostilities were suspended pending the arrival of these, and, as they rode up, the threatening and tumultuous clamour was changed into deep-toned salutations addressed to the chief.

The latter was a well-built elderly man, with no insignia of chieftainship about him, not even the thick ivory armlet which he wore just above the left elbow, for several of his followers wore this adornment too. But the deference displayed towards him by this unruly mob, that told its own tale. For such is the prestige and authority of a tribal chief among the Amaxosa that if you have him on your side in any dispute with his subjects, why, the matter is settled. That now Usivulele was upon our side I had no doubt, seeing that Brian was riding with him. The other two were old men with grizzled heads, and were *amapakati*, or councillors. Way was at once made for the group, and a rush to hold their horses as they dismounted.

"I see a chief," said Septimus Matterson in figurative greeting—he had already put away his revolver, and so had I, with a feeling of relief it would be impossible to exaggerate. "Now we can talk."

"My heart is very sore over what has happened, my friend," he went on. "Yet he who has done this thing is a child, and he has done it by accident. When a child does that for which a grown man would be killed, he is not killed because he is only a child. He is not killed, but he is punished. Is it not so?"

The three uttered a murmur of assent. Brian said nothing.

"Well, then, although this thing was an accident, and although the child is my own son, I do not propose to shield him from punishment. But it is not for me, and it is not for these here, to decide on what punishment he shall receive. It is for the law. Therefore I am going to send to Fort Lamport for the *amapolise*, and the boy will be taken to the magistrate there. After that we must leave him to the laws of the Government. Say. Is not that just and fair?"

"*Ewa*," assented the three, and I observed that a like murmur went up from not a few in the listening crowd.

"*Hau!*" broke forth one voice. "What of our father, Kuliso? Those who are killed were of his house."

The interruption had proceeded from Sibuko. The hulking ruffian, standing there in the forefront, his muscular frame smeared from head to foot with red ochre, a vengeful sneer upon his savage face as he significantly gripped his kerries, struck me as about as evil and formidable an impersonation of barbarism as it would be possible to present.

"Yes. What of our father, Kuliso?" echoed others. But Usivulele merely waved a hand, and there was silence as by magic.

"You all know me, *amadoda*," went on Septimus Matterson. "Now I will write a letter to the magistrate, and two of your number shall carry it. By to-night the *amapolise* will be here."

"*Hau!* The *amapolise* will be here. But will the boy be here?" said the abominable Sibuko, with his head craftily on one side.

"You can see for yourselves. Let some of you watch the house until the *amapolise* arrive."

"But how do we know he is here now?" went on this persistent savage. "He may have been taken away quietly during all this time. Bring him out, and let us see him."

"*Ewa, ewa!*" shouted several.

This would have been acceded to, when a sudden instinct of the impolicy of such a course flashed across my mind, and I take a sneaking pride in having supplemented judgment to so experienced and judicious a mind when for once that attribute seemed to fail.

"Don't you do it," I said hurriedly and in an undertone. "No point in making the boy too *marked*, under the circumstances. Show him to the chief only."

"You're right, Kenrick." Then aloud: "The chief will satisfy you. He will come into my house and see the boy."

While this was being done Brian quickly put me up to his own movements. There was no doubt about it but that two of the Kafir boys were dead. It was a most lamentable and unfortunate affair for everybody concerned. How had he fallen in with Usivulele? Ah, that was something of a piece of luck. He had got wind of a dangerous demonstration being organised, had seen the Kafirs swarming along the hillsides from different points, but all converging upon the same—our valley to wit. Only one way to counteract this had suggested itself, and accordingly he had ridden straight and hard for Usivulele's kraal. He and his were on exceedingly friendly terms with that chief, and he had soon prevailed upon him to intervene.

"Well, Brian, if ever a man did the right thing at the right time, you did it then. A few minutes later would have been so many minutes too late."

"I believe so," he said. "I could see that things were looking as ugly as they could. Well, it'll be all right now, at least as far as Kuliso's people are concerned."

Then Usivulele came forth again, and began haranguing the crowd. The whole thing was as had been said, he informed them, and they might now go home. The matter was in his hands now, and he would remain until the boy was handed over to the *amopolise*. This he himself would see done. Then he chose two men to carry the letter in to Fort Lamport, and the crowd began to break up. A few manifested a disposition to hang around and see the thing out, and this was not objected to, but the remainder scattered off in groups, or by twos and threes, and glad indeed we were to see the last of them.

It may be imagined what a gloom there was over us all during the remainder of that day. Beryl hardly appeared, and George not at all, and even poor little Iris had lost her sunny flow of spirits. We three men had hardly the heart for anything, and got through time chatting with the chief and his councillors, who, incidentally, were lavishly entertained. But it was not until late at night that a squad of Mounted Police arrived, under a sergeant, to take charge of the boy.

We were not sorry to learn either from the same source that a strong patrol would be working along this side of Kuliso's location, for it was arranged that we should all start for Fort Lamport together at daybreak.

Chapter Twenty One.

In Court.

Shattuck, C.C. and R.M., was not a genial type of Civil servant, in that he was cold and short of manner, and always intensely official. Moreover, he was popularly credited with a strong native bias, which alone was sufficient to constitute him a round peg in a square hole, in a frontier magistracy such as Fort Lamport. Personally, he was a middle-aged man with a high bald forehead, and wearing a light full beard—would have been a good-looking one but for a normally acid expression of countenance.

Poor George stood limply in the dock, all the cheek taken out of him, as Brian and I had laughingly told him, as we tried all we knew to hearten him up just before he was placed there. Indeed, there were not wanting those who thought ill of the magistrate's curt refusal of our attorney's application to allow him to stand beside his father throughout the preliminary examination, on account of his youth.

"I cannot make such exceptions as that, Mr Pyle," had been the answer. "Had it been the case of a native no such application would have been made."

This, by the way, was the sort of remark which did not precisely tend to enhance Shattuck's popularity.

The Courthouse was a dingy, stuffy little enclosure, and it was crowded to overflowing, the back part of the room, usually occupied by natives, being closely packed with dark faces and rolling eyeballs; but scattered among the townspeople was a large number of stock farmers, many of whom had travelled considerable distances in order to render the Mattersons a kind of moral support.

The first called was the District Surgeon, who made a post-mortem of the two bodies. The deceased, he deposed, were boys of about fifteen or sixteen, as far as he could judge. Then he proceeded to technical detail, such as the number of shot-wounds in each, when and where placed, and so forth. As to the other two who were wounded, he, the District Surgeon, could not say they were out of danger yet. Their injuries were undoubtedly severe.

Then followed, severally, the three or four boys who had been in the company of those shot, and at the time. These gave their version of the affair pretty much as George had given his. He had abused them for being there, they said, and ordered them away. They laughed at him, and he called out that if they did not go at once he would shoot them. He was pointing his gun at them at the time, and the next thing they knew was that it went off and four of them were lying on the ground. The remainder ran away.

The tale of each tallied, but Pyle, the attorney who was watching the case on behalf of George, after a bit of a wrangle with the Court interpreter as to the exact shade of meaning which the order to move on would or would not bear in the native vernacular, fastened upon two points in cross-examination. One was the distance between the slayer and slain, but there was no room for doubt here. He was on the top of the cliff while they were beneath it. But it was not a high one. How high? As high as the Court room?—Higher, perhaps twice as high. Obviously any one shooting at that short distance would be shooting to kill, not merely to frighten. Even a boy who was accustomed to firearms, like George was, and however careless, could be under no mistake on that head. This to dispose of any idea that he had intended merely to "pepper" the deceased without intent seriously to wound.

The other point upon which our attorney harped was the demeanour of the accused. Was he angry when he ordered them away?—Yes. He said they were spoiling his hunt. Did they seriously think he meant to shoot them when he threatened to?—Well, they didn't know. But if anybody points a gun at you and you think he means to shoot you, you don't stand still and laugh at him?—*Whau*! They hadn't thought of it in that light. No, they supposed he had not intended to shoot. Then it had been an accident?—Yes, they supposed so.

All this was put by Pyle to the witnesses in due order, and they were unanimous in their answers. Pyle was radiant. During the slight commotion of finding the next witness he leaned back and whispered to us—

"He'll be discharged. Even Shattuck can't send him for trial on top of that admission."

All the same, we were not quite so sure.

Then was led a good deal of Kafir evidence, that of parents and other relatives of the dead boys, but this dealt mainly with identification, and was of little or no value for or against our side. It was tediously drawn out too by reason of the interpreting, and was not completed by the time the Court adjourned for lunch.

"Buck up, old chap," said Pyle, going over to poor George, who was not allowed to leave with us. "Buck up. You'll be having it with your governor next grub time."

"Thanks, Mr Pyle, but I don't believe I shall," was the doleful reply as he was taken into the chief constable's room to devour some sandwiches which Beryl had sent him.

As we passed out of the dingy hall into the glare of the sunlight, the contrast was a relief. It was good to be out in the open air again, but the contrast was sharper as we thought of the poor boy we had just left. What if imprisonment, even for a comparatively short time, was before him?

The native end of the Courthouse had emptied out its malodorous crowd, but this was nothing to the number of those who had been unable to gain admission, for to-day the whole township seemed to grow Kafirs, who had come in from near and far by reason of the excitement of the case. Some were squatting around in groups, lustily discussing it; others lounging around the general stores; while others again were shaping a course for the nearest canteen. All had sticks, and not a few a pair of them.

"The sooner they pass a bye-law against carrying kerries in the streets the better," said Brian, as we walked over to the hotel. "There are enough of these chaps here to-day to take the town if they made up their minds. Hullo!"

The last was evoked by the sound of a great voice haranguing one of the groups we were passing. Looking round, we recognised Sibuko.

This pestilent savage was squatting on his haunches, holding forth volubly, emphasising his points with a flourish of his kerrie in the air, or bringing it down with a whack on the ground. But to me he was of secondary interest beside a face in the group that caught my eye.

"Brian, twig that chap three doors off from Sibuko," I said hurriedly. "That's the one who was going to cut my throat in the cave that morning. By Jove! I wonder if he remembers the knock-out I gave him. I wouldn't mind repeating it either."

"Well, you can't—not here and now. In the first place, there are too many of them; in the next, Shattuck would fine you about twenty pounds; and thirdly, we don't want to stir up that stew over again."

The hotel was pretty full, and the first person to catch my eye as we entered the dining-room, rather late, was that infernal Trask, who had calmly appropriated the seat next to Beryl, and which I had mentally marked out for myself. Moreover, he was in train of trying to be excessively funny, which was his way of keeping everybody's spirits up.

"Hallo, Holt," he sang out. "Got your seat, I'm afraid. We'd given you up. Plenty of room down there, old chap. By the way, how are things going?"

"Well, we think," I answered curtly, moving to the vacant part at the far end of the room.

"Ha-ha! Holt seems a bit raggy to-day about something," I distinctly heard Trask say. "What an uncertain tempered Johnny he is."

But I did not hear Beryl's reply, and—I should have liked to.

We had to hurry back to court again, and, the native evidence concluded, Brian was called to the witness-box. He deposed to George's return home directly after the tragedy, and how he and I were the first to hear the boy's account of the same, and from that, his first account, he had never swerved in any detail. Also how he himself had proceeded to the scene of the tragedy in the hope of being of some aid. Pyle then questioned him about the accused's disposition. Was he inclined to be careless with firearms?

No, Brian didn't think he was. All boys were more or less careless about most things. Whereat a titter ran through the crowd.

Was the accused of a mischievous disposition?

"Not more than most other boys of his age." And at this the titter became a laugh, causing the magistrate, whose official soul was scandalised, to glance up sharply.

Was he of a passionate or vindictive disposition?

"Not in the least," answered Brian decisively. "I am as convinced that the whole affair was a sheer accident—the thoughtless pointing of a gun at anybody I don't defend—as I am that I stand here at this moment."

A murmur of applause greeted this remark, and then Brian being done with, I was invited to take his place, but as all that was wanted from me was a mere confirmation of George's first narrative of the affair, I soon got down again.

Septimus Matterson followed. He was very much affected, but gave his evidence in a sensible straightforward manner that was worthy of all praise. He told of the irruption of indignant natives on to his place, but without any rancour or ill-will. As for the accident, no one regretted and deplored it more than he did, unless it was his unfortunate son, and he fully intended, according to Kafir custom in the matter of homicide, to make liberal compensation to the relatives of the slain boys. As to which he would be glad if the magistrate would allow this to be made known by the interpreter for the satisfaction of the natives at the back of the court.

He had always lived on friendly terms with his Kafir neighbours, he went on when the hum of applause that greeted the last announcement had subsided, and hoped always to do so, in spite of this deplorable accident; several of their chiefs, too, were well known to and esteemed by him and his, and now in this case he had been the first to surrender up his own son to justice.

"That will do, Mr Matterson," said Pyle hurriedly, seeing signs of an utter breakdown. And he beckoned him from the box.

Then he began a fervid appeal to the Bench. If all the testimony they had just listened to was worth a jot, he said, it was clear as clear could be that the case was not one of culpable homicide or of manslaughter, but of accidental death. The evidence of the native witnesses, fair and straightforward as, to their great credit, it had been, made this way, even more if possible than that of the relatives and friends of the accused. The only eyewitnesses of the tragedy, besides the accused, had frankly admitted when it was put fairly to them, that the lamentable and deplorable affair must have been an accident.

Then he went on to enlarge upon the terrible mental punishment this boy— this mere child—had already undergone, a consciousness which would last far into his after and maturer life, of what one act of carelessness had involved; and having expatiated thus and at some length, concluded by pathetically urging his worship to discharge the accused, and not to add further to his own sufferings and to those of his sorrowing relatives.

There was dead silence as the attorney ended this appeal. We, and indeed all in the room, took for granted that it would bear fruit, and that George's discharge would follow. But we reckoned without Shattuck.

"As Mr Pyle has observed," began the magistrate, "this is a painful and deplorable case. Even an accident may have its culpable features, rendering its perpetrator amenable to the law. Here two lives have been sacrificed owing to a most culpable piece of thoughtless bravado on the part of the accused, and I should not be doing my duty in summarily discharging him. It is a case for a judge and jury to decide, and the accused stands committed to the next Circuit Court here."

Then the formality of asking him if he wished to make a statement being gone through, and having been duly cautioned, George, instructed by the attorney, repeated, "It was an accident," and in a scrawling, shaky, schoolboy hand signed his statement.

Then Pyle applied that bail should be granted. There was plenty of substantial security available, he added. And at his words at least a dozen men stood up. But the next words that fell from the Bench were even a greater thunderbolt to us than the decision to commit.

"I cannot grant bail, Mr Pyle."

"Not grant bail, your worship?"

"No. Not in a case of this nature."

"But there's no more substantial man in the district than the boy's father, your worship."

"I am far from denying it. But—I cannot grant bail."

Quite an angry murmur ran through the audience at this. But the magistrate merely looked up.

"Several persons here are committing a very distinct contempt of court," he observed coldly. "Remove the prisoner."

The poor little chap kept up bravely till he was out of sight. Then he broke down and fairly howled.

To do Shattuck justice, his apparent hard-heartedness was not without motive, for on the rising of the Court—that is to say immediately, for there were no more cases that day—he asked us to step into his office.

"I am very grieved, Mr Matterson, over the course I have been obliged to take," he began, stiffly and constrainedly, "but I fully believe I am serving your best interests in doing as I have done. If the boy were given back to you now, would not all the Kafirs around, and Kuliso's people in particular, at once jump to the conclusion that justice had not been done, and that there was one law for the black and another for the white? In short, I believe his life would be in hourly danger. Their demonstration on your farm seems to point that way, doesn't it? Well now, if they know he is here in prison—I am not going to have him put in an ordinary cell, by the way—they will be to that extent satisfied, and it will give any strong feelings time to die down a bit. The case is out of my hands now. The records will be forwarded immediately to the Solicitor-General, and of course it rests with him whether the matter goes any further."

There was sound sense in this, and indeed the magistrate had shown a consideration we had not expected from him. So we parted good friends, and rather arriving at the conclusion that Shattuck was not such a bad sort of fellow after all.

Chapter Twenty Two.

Kuliso's "Great Place."

Gonya's kloof seemed no longer the same place. The period of suspense following upon George's committal told upon all of us, seeming to cast a gloom over everything, damping our spirits. Of myself especially did this hold good, for Beryl was no longer there. She and Iris had remained in Fort Lamport after the preliminary examination staying with friends, and we three men were alone.

What a difference it made! During the months I had already spent on the place, Beryl had never been absent for a single day, and now that presence which had rendered the hardest of toil sweet, and irradiated the norm of the daily round with a glow that seemed hardly of earth—to myself, that is—was now removed. Yet the sun shone just as brightly and the generous riches of Nature expanded around with the same fairness to eye and sense; but—to myself—all lay as beneath the shadow of a cloud.

Many times a day would I recall the keenness of the pang when she had told us of her intention to remain in the town for the present. The announcement was made in the presence of several persons, or there was no telling how I might have taken it. As it was, I have a confused recollection of turning on a vacuous grin, and hoping she would enjoy her stay; which was about as idiotic a rejoinder as even I could have been guilty of, considering that a state of anxious suspense would be the family portion for perhaps weeks to come. Well, she had removed her presence from among us, and to me it seemed that all the savour had gone out of life. And if this was so during a matter of days or weeks, what would it mean if extended throughout life?

This consideration had rather a maddening effect. Why had I not boldly tried my chances before, instead of shilly-shallying around until the opportunity had passed? Our acquaintance was no longer a thing of a day, and as for circumstances, others had started in life—or in a new line, which amounts to the same thing—under far fewer advantages, material, physical or prospective, than I enjoyed, and had made a good thing of it. That hideous and constitutional reticence of mine had stood in the way, I now saw; yet even then I had been on the point of putting matters to the test on the very day before the tragical event which seemed to have changed the whole course of our daily life, when that infernal Trask had blundered his obtrusive presence in upon us, according to his wont. Now it was too late. Obviously under present circumstances the time would be in the highest degree unfavourable.

I have a recollection, too, at that period, of going through sundry phases of insanity. For instance, I would sit for quite a long time, when in the company of others, and say nothing; the fact being that I was simply giving the rein to thought, of course only in the one direction. Of this phase I was cured, mainly through the agency of the abominable Trask, whose horse banter and innuendo at such times rendered it difficult to keep my hands off him. However, it had a tonic effect, in that it caused me to pull myself together. But I was much addicted to straying in the direction of various spots where Beryl and I had been alone together, and, letting imagination have free rein, would conjure up her sweet bright presence, so alluringly framed by the wild beauty of the surroundings, illumined by the sunlit glow of the cloudless heaven; would go over our conversations together, utterly trivial and unmomentous as such might have been. To half a hundred other and minor idiocies do I likewise plead guilty; but as I have reason to believe that my lot was by no means singular, and that most of us are fated to undergo a similar stage of imbecility at any rate once in our lives, such belief is fraught with some comfort.

Further, the parlous state into which I had mentally fallen affected my ordinary duties, and what had hitherto been performed with a wholehearted zest now became tedious and wearisome. That is the worst of physical labour, in that you can *think* throughout it all. Here my natural reticence, or caution perhaps, came to the rescue. I began to wonder whether Brian or his father saw through my state of mind. If so they gave no sign. But I must pull myself together; and did so.

I have not unfrequently had occasion to notice how rarely anybody is allowed in this life to suffer from a repletion of contentment over-long. Here was this household, including myself, leading a life which, in a modest way, left absolutely nothing to wish for: a life of healthful, congenial usefulness, yet, thanks to the characteristics of its individuals, not one of stagnation by any means. Then this blow had fallen—suddenly, as serious blows generally do. Even if matters ended at the best we could hope for, the occurrence would leave its mark, and things could not, at any rate for a long time, be just as before. We three men, left alone, realised a good deal of this. There was a gloom upon us, checking our usual free flow of conversation, as though we were each and all trying to avoid the topic uppermost in our minds, or at any rate in the minds of two of us.

One day we rode over to Kuliso's "Great Place," to arrange about the compensation to be delivered to the chief for the death of the children, according to native custom. It was a strange expedition, and one by no means free from danger; for apart from the bad reputation of Kuliso and his clan, there was again unrest on the border—unrest which was deepening day by day, so, although ostensibly unarmed, each of us had a loaded revolver in his right hand pocket. A strange expedition indeed, its object a barter over the price of human life; and if such failed, what about we three in the midst of hundreds, if not thousands, of brooding savages, in ugly and vindictive mood? But Septimus Matterson declared he had never been afraid of Kafirs, and did not intend to make a start in that line now. Yet I, for my part, as we took our way through the Ndhlambe location—with miles of kraals on either hand, studding the veldt far and wide, whose dusky denizens turned out at sight of us, following on our steps near and far to see what went on over at the Great Place—why, I found myself devoutly hoping we might be suffered to return as we had come.

The chief, Kuliso, was a tall, broad, finely built man in the prime of life, with, for a Kafir, quite a heavily bearded face. It was a strong face, too, with its lofty forehead and air of command, but it was a crafty and unreliable one. Around him squatted a dozen or so of much older men, grey-bearded and wizened—being, in fact, his *amapakati*, or councillors. All wore no other clothing than an ample blanket, stained red with ochre, carelessly draped around the body, and for adornment most of them, including the chief, had a splendid armlet of solid white ivory just above the left elbow. With an eye to artistic effect it occurred to me that the group, with their shrewd dark faces and unconscious grace of attitude, against the background of domed huts, and the increasing groups of Kafirs clustering up from all sides, their reddened frames in contrast against the green of the veldt and the yellow thatch of the huts, would have made no mean subject for the artist's paint-brush.

But little scope was there for the indulgence of artistic imaginings, for the day was destined to be long and trying. Septimus Matterson, speaking fluently and at length, yes, even pathetically—for I had learned enough of the Xosa tongue by that time to be able to follow him, roughly, through most of his arguments to recognise that much—recapitulated all the sad circumstances. If these had brought sorrow to the House of Kuliso, he said, they had hardly brought less to his own house; and Brian and I, listening, were inclined to believe they had brought more. However, after some further roundabout talk, mostly of an apologetic nature—for savages never appreciate a direct coming to the point—he made them an offer, and one, even under the circumstances, and from their point of custom, of exceptional liberality.

But it was not appreciated, let alone jumped at. "The sense of the meeting"— to use a civilised and newspaper phrase—was nasty. The chief, who in actual fact cared no more for the lives that had been taken than had they been those of so many jackals, save that they represented a substantial addition to his own wealth under the current negotiations, held forth in unctuous strain upon the value of life, and the grief of the dead ones' relatives, and so forth, his words being emphasised by deep-toned exclamations from the *amapakati*, which were echoed almost in a shout by the surrounding crowd. Thus encouraged, he concluded by demanding a payment which would have crippled the Mattersons—well-to-do as they were—seriously for many years.

"This is too much," came the reply, clear and decided, and in the tone of a man who knew he was being grossly imposed upon. "I have other children besides this one who is now in the hands of the law. I cannot rob them, and I will not. Now take this or leave it, for it is all I will give." And he doubled his original offer.

The jeering hoot that arose among the bystanders died away to silence, for the chief and the *amapakati* were consulting. It was a strange scene, this question of barter over human lives—a strange scene, and a weird one. Some hours had already been spent in the negotiations, and now the sky had become partly overcast, and in the background a great curtain of opaque inky cloud had arisen, against whose blackness jets of lightning were luridly playing, and ever and anon a heavy booming roll. Then in the silence a curious deep drumming sound was heard. All eyes were turned upward, as overhead flapped several large birds, and in the ungainly black shapes and long sabre-like beaks we recognised the *brom-vogel*, or large hornbill of South Africa, which, by the way, plays its part in native superstitions. On flapped the birds, slowly winging their way right over the kraal, their deep, heavy note mingling with the approaching thunder roll. Yes. It was a strange picture— the unearthly, boding stillness, the livid cloud lit up by lightning gleams, the tall red forms of the clustering barbarians, the upturned eyeballs, the awed hush as some murmured of witchcraft and omens, the chief and councillors grouped in earnest debate, and the background of yellow domes against a dark and angry sky. There was a tension about it that got upon my nerves, and I said as much to Brian.

He, for answer, got out his pipe, slowly filled and lighted it, then sent a deliberate look upwards and around, as though the state of the weather occupied his sole consideration. At that moment my glance fell upon one face among the bystanders, and I could only just repress a start, for it was that of the English-speaking rascal whose kind intentions towards myself in the cattle-stealers' den I had so violently and effectually frustrated. He, of course, had recognised me from the first, but now as our glances met, the glare of hate and menace upon his repulsive countenance deepened, and without taking his gaze from mine he said something to those who stood next him which caused them to regard me too with an expression the very reverse of benevolent. There was something uncomfortable in the way this fellow kept on turning up—the other day in Fort Lamport, now again here. I felt sure that he would lay himself out to be even with me for the rough treatment he had met with, though in the first instance he had brought it upon himself, and in the second—well, it was to save my own life.

Now at last the negotiations had come to an end; to our intense relief satisfactorily so. Kuliso had accepted the terms, only stipulating that a few unconsidered trifles, such as rolls of tobacco, blankets, etc., should be thrown in as *basela*, which was readily agreed to. Then there was great shaking of hands as the chief and some of his *amapakati* got up and accompanied us to where our horses were being held for us.

"*Au*! This is a new white man," said Kuliso, with a grin, enclosing my hand within his sinewy grip. He was taller than me, and I am not short, and as he thus confronted me, and I took in the fine proportions and strong yet sinister countenance of this great muscular savage, it was with feelings of repulsion and distrust, for all *the* geniality he was striving to exhibit. For I had an instinctive idea we should similarly confront one another again, and that under inauspicious circumstances. But how strange and terrible those circumstances were destined to be, I had then little if any idea.

Chapter Twenty Three.

Good News—and some Bad.

"Here comes a fellow who looks as if he didn't want to use his horse again for a day or two." And Brian shaded his eyes to watch a moving speck rapidly approaching, but still at a considerable distance.

The hour was just before sunrise, a couple of mornings after our visit to Kuliso, and the two of us were standing on the stoep drinking our early cup of coffee.

"Why, it's Revell," he went on, as a look through the field-glasses revealed the identity of the horseman, now lost to sight, now reappearing round a bend of the hillside. "You can see the flaming halo around his face, even from here. By jingo! I hope there's nothing wrong. He's going at a hard gallop. Look, dad," he called through the window. "Come out. Here's Revell coming up the kloof at such a pace you'd think the joker whose name rhymes with his was after him."

"Perhaps he's bringing us some news," was the answer. "Well, well! We ought to be ready for anything."

The dogs charged forward with open-mouthed clamour to greet the advancing hoof-strokes, and in a few minutes the horseman dashed up to the stoep.

"News!" he shouted. "News for you!"

"Bad, I suppose?" said Septimus Matterson.

"No. Good. First-rate."

Even while dismounting he had been fumbling in his pocket, and now held out a long blue envelope. I believed I could see the recipient's fingers slightly tremble as he tore open this, but his voice was firm enough as he read out its contents, which set forward in terse official phraseology that *in re* The Queen *versus* George Matterson, the Solicitor-General, having examined the evidence, did not consider the facts such as to warrant a criminal prosecution, and that the said George Matterson had been released accordingly, and handed over to the care of his sister. The writer then had the honour to be the recipient's obedient servant, John Shattuck, Resident Magistrate.

"Hip—hip—hooray!" whooped Revell, flourishing his hat in the air, a proceeding which caused his steed, which was standing, veldt-fashion, with merely the end of the bridle resting on the ground, to throw up its head and trot away down the kloof again, snorting vehemently, and the dogs to assail him with frantic energy of purpose which nearly bore disastrous fruit.

"You are a good chap to bring us the news, Revell," said Brian. "*Magtig, kerel!* but you've ridden your horse to death!"

"Well, it was good enough, wasn't it? Bliss Matterson was keen on letting you know at once, but couldn't get hold of any one coming out this way, so I volunteered. I said I'd be the first to bring the news, and I have," concluded this prince of good fellows quite delightedly.

"Now come inside and have some scoff," said Brian. "I'll send and have your gee looked after. You must have ridden all night."

"So I did. What of it? You'd do as much for Miss Beryl, wouldn't you? Man, but the nipper was jolly glad to get out of the *tronk*, I can tell you. Shattuck had no business ever to have put him in. He bust out howling when Miss Beryl went to fetch him."

"Who did? Shattuck?" I said.

"Eh? Oh, shut up, Holt. Don't you try to come the Trask," was the chuckling retort. "By the way, Mr Matterson—what a blundering ass I am—here's a *brievje* from Miss Beryl. Oh, and I brought out your post while I was about it."

Beryl's note was merely a repetition of the official intimation, and was coupled with a request that some one should come in to Fort Lamport as soon as possible to fetch them out. She judged it better to come home at once.

No one thought of taking notice at that moment of anything so trivial as the mere weekly post. The two or three letters for myself I put in my pocket, hardly glancing at the addresses. Business, of course, but not of urgent importance. On a day like this it could keep.

It was decided that Brian should start with the Cape cart soon after breakfast. He would be at Fort Lamport early in the afternoon, and could even come out nearly half way to-night, and if they did that, and slept at a friend's farm, why, they would all be back by this time to-morrow.

To these arrangements I listened as in a trance. Beryl would be with us again. This time to-morrow! Why, it was hardly credible. It seemed a year since we had been without her. Not even until this time to-morrow would *I* wait, however, for already I was busy formulating a little scheme of my own for riding out at some perfectly ungodly hour of the early morning to meet them. Ah, now everything was coming right. It was like a story, by Jove it was; and now this time I would not let the grass grow under my feet. Why should I, indeed? Everything had gone well. Kuliso and his clan were satisfied with their compensation. George was liberated. The only thing to do was to try and forget the whole unfortunate affair all round. And, I hoped—very strongly hoped—I would soon be in a position to help one of them at any rate duly to forget it.

What an ultra-celestial gleam there was in the newly-risen sun, which had now just soared free of the further hills, deepening the cloudless blue into a richer depth! What a ring of joyousness in the varying bird notes, tossed from spray to spray and from tree to tree, over the wide free expanse! Even the distant voices of the farm Kafirs, and the bleat of the flocks, seemed to my wrought-up brain to take on a very gladsomeness of tone. By that time to-morrow Beryl would be home again, and even before then I should have seen her, sweet, fresh and radiant in the rose-glow of the early morning.

All this ran through my mind, and kept me silent; but there was no need to talk, for Revell was a host in himself in that line, and now he was launching forth by the hour, mostly as to the affair which had just met with so fortunate a conclusion, unflattering comments upon the laws of the Colony in general, and their administrator, Shattuck, in particular. Then, after an early breakfast, Brian inspanned, and with a few parting injunctions from his father, drove off.

Revell, naturally enough, was in no hurry to move on, and in my then mood his ceaseless, if harmless, chatter annoyed me. There was nothing particular to be done about the homestead, so I saddled up a horse for a ride round the veldt. I might get a shot at something, but that was a secondary consideration. I wanted to be alone and think.

Very rose-tinted was the reverie in which I was wrapped, as my steed paced on, over swelling rise or through bushed valley bottom. I went back over all the time I had spent in this happy home. I thought of her whose presence had brightened it, and called to mind all manner of little circumstances which now stood out in anything but a discouraging light. Why, even to-morrow might decide everything, given the opportunity, and that I would endeavour to make. And somehow or other I felt strangely buoyant as to the result.

For all the use I made of it I might as well have left my gun at home, yet it was for no lack of chances. A pair of vaal koorhaans rose almost beneath the horse's feet—rare chance indeed at these wary and beautiful birds, themselves all too scarce in our locality—yet I merely watched them as they winged their way out of shot, uttering their querulous note. Further on, a duiker ram, slinking along not thirty yards distant, a shot I could not have missed, yet I let him go. Later again a large troop of guinea-fowl running for a prickly pear *klompje*, where, had I followed them up, I should have been sure of at least a brace. They too were left unmolested. The wild game of the veldt seemed to be under a kind of "truce of God." As far as I was concerned, I felt disinclined to take life that day.

I had reached the spot where I had shot my first bush-buck ram, somewhat lower down in the Zwaart Kloof from the scene of the subsequent tragedy, and here it occurred to me that I would dismount and smoke a quiet pipe; in pursuance of which idea, feeling in my pocket for my pouch, my hand came in contact with the letters I had put there that morning, still unopened and totally forgotten. They were from England, but probably of no importance— possibly some further and tedious delay as to the transfer of my capital, but there was no such violent hurry about that.

The first mystified me, but very uncomfortably so. I believe my hand shook as I tore open the second, and then—and then—I could feel myself growing white and cold—everything was going round. A blow on the head could hardly have stunned me more. For, before I got half through the contents of that horrible communication, I realised the hideous fact. I was a ruined man. The solicitors to whom had been entrusted the transfer of my capital had defaulted for a huge amount, an amount beside which my little all was a mere sixpence, and every farthing of the said "little all" was in their hands. Beyond a few pounds in the bank at Fort Lamport, and the value of the few head of stock I had running on the place, I was penniless.

I stared at the hateful characters of the communication and shrank from reading it again. Yet I did so, and by its light the first I had opened stood explained. It was too explicit. The whole had vanished—vanished utterly. Not even a halfpenny in the pound would any composition afford.

What of the golden dream in which, but a moment ago it seemed, I had been enwrapped? What of the happy, healthful, independent life I had been mapping out? And, of course, what of Beryl?

All—all had vanished. No more thought of independence for me. As a man without means I must be at the beck and call of others, content that way merely to earn a livelihood. No more thought of love. That was a luxury as far beyond me now as a country seat or a town house. The rose-hued dream must disappear, dispelled by an irruption of dank and gloomy fog. I was practically a beggar.

Beryl was coming home to-morrow, but to me that meant nothing now. Yet how could I go through the anguish of dwelling beneath the same roof with her day after day, month after month, knowing that she was lost to me, for, of course, now I could never tell her. And then, as if to render the mockery more diabolically complete, a sort of consciousness came over me that had I spoken sooner she would have refused now to give me back my troth. She was of the stuff who would stand by a man through ill as well as through good. Well, it was too late now. The opportunity had gone—gone for ever.

Had this blow overtaken me earlier, or even now had I never known Beryl Matterson, it would have been bad enough. Now it had fallen with tenfold force—with a force that crushed. A wild eerie temptation came over me, as my glance rested upon the gun which stood against a boulder. This kloof had so recently witnessed one tragedy, why not another? There was nothing left in life, and in my then frame of mind I could imagine nothing worse in the hereafter than the veritable agony I was now undergoing. Indeed, so sharp was the temptation that I have a recollection of resolutely throwing all my cartridges over the krantz. Further, I remember walking with a sort of dazed stagger as I made my way over to where my horse had strayed some twenty yards, and was placidly cropping the grass, the bridle trailing on the ground.

Well, the situation had to be faced. I must pull myself together and make the best of it—which sounds an excellent, hard-headed, common sense, even cheery, way of looking at things, as a theory. At any rate, I kept repeating it over and over again to myself during that homeward ride and afterwards. But, alternating with it, in jangling refrain, was gloomy, hopeless, desperate fact— Ruined! Penniless! Beggared!

Chapter Twenty Four.

Turns of the Knife.

"Hullo, Kenrick. What's the row?" sang out Brian, even before he had got down from the driving seat. "Man, but you do look sick."

"He just does," echoed Iris from the back, herself as yet hardly visible.

A stranger who had been seated beside Brian now got down.

"Mr Holt, isn't it?" he said. "Glad to meet you. I've heard so much about you."

The address was frank and friendly, the aspect of the speaker prepossessing. I strove to respond with suitable cordiality, and while doing so a resolve flashed lightning-like through my mind. I was giving myself away by dwelling too much on this direful change. Well, I would not.

"Oh, I'm all jolly," I said, with forced carelessness. "Think I got a touch of the sun yesterday. All right again now."

The while I was helping to extract the other occupants of the Cape cart—first Iris, then Beryl. Her quick, solicitous glance as we clasped hands was not lost on me, nor was the tact wherewith she refrained from adding her comments upon my personal appearance. Then George got himself out, looking very sobered and subdued, and quite different to the impudent mischievous pup of so short a while back.

"Where's the dad?" said Brian, looking up from his outspanning. "He's not seedy, too, is he?"

"Not a bit. He's down in the further land. Ah, here he comes. By Jove, Brian, you've had rather a load," I went on, as I helped in the extraction of numerous bundles, and in the casting loose of the luggage lashed on behind. I must be doing something, I felt; talking too, otherwise the contrast between this return as I had pictured it hardly twenty-four hours ago and as it now was, would have been too forcibly brought home. Then, even though others were by, I would have managed to convey to Beryl what a delight her return had brought to, at any rate, myself; now, we had met in ordinary conventional fashion, and she was chatting with the stranger, while I chaffed Iris and tried to cheer up that poor little devil, George.

The stranger aforesaid, whose name was Pentridge, was a well-set-up, good-looking fellow of about my own age, a man to whom under other circumstances I should have taken. But now it was easy to see that Beryl occupied nearly, if not quite, as large a preponderance in his thoughts as she did in mine. He was a doctor by profession, and an old acquaintance of the

Mattersons, though they had not met for some time. Now, meeting him by chance in Fort Lamport, Beryl had invited him out to the farm.

Here was a new element in the situation for which I had not bargained. The said situation I had thought out again and again during the twenty-four hours which had intervened since my first hearing the abominable news, and notably during an almost sleepless night. I would not say anything about it yet; would take time to think it over more fully. Meanwhile I had found some comfort in the thought that things would be to all outward appearance as they had been. Beryl and I would be together as before; and did I, by any chance, cherish a wild vague hope that anything might happen to cut the knot of the whole difficulty? I believe I did.

But now the advent of this stranger upset all this. In him I saw a rival, and a potent one, for he was probably in a position to declare himself at any moment, while I must perforce lie low. Not only this, but there was that in the personality of the fellow which rendered him doubly dangerous, for he was one of those men to whom all women would naturally turn, some indeed with headlong resistless attraction; whereas I, Kenrick Holt—plain, common-place, plodding—knew myself to be endowed with no such attributes, and had anybody hinted to the contrary, should have laughed in their face.

Upon the resolve to keep my own counsel for the present followed another one, and this was to throw off the dead weight which the change in my fortunes had at first bound upon me, outwardly at any rate. Wherefore as we all shook down again into the ordinary routine of life, I avoided any appearance of aloofness and strove to bear myself as if there had been no change at all. But it involved a tremendous effort of will, amounting at times almost to physical anguish. For instance, if we were taking a collective walk or ride, and I had to witness the incidental pairing off together of Beryl and Pentridge, the bitter reflection that up till now it would have been her and myself would require some crushing down, it may safely be assumed; or in half a hundred incidents of everyday life he had a way of showing her little attentions, and that in a way which to me, at any rate, was unmistakable, though there was this about Pentridge, he never trod upon his own heels, so to say, with over-eagerness.

Still, my manner towards her must have undergone an unconscious change, for more than once Beryl would give me a strange look which I could not quite fathom. Sometimes, too, she would take on almost a coldness towards me, as different from her former free, unaffected cordiality as it could possibly be. Ah! a light suddenly dawned upon me. I was in the way, was becoming a nuisance to her. And acting upon this idea, I threw myself into the work of the place with tenfold energy. That would keep me out pretty well all day, and every day—but then, there was always the evening.

To me there was a humorous element underlying even this situation, and it spelt Trask. Trask's disgust on finding Pentridge already in the field was quite comical. He could no longer monopolise the conversation, and when he started in to be funny, Pentridge, without seeming to do so, would invariably cap his would-be wit, and effectually turn it against himself. In short, to use a homely metaphor, Trask's nose was put clean out of joint.

"Who the deuce is that bounder Pentridge, Holt?" he said to me one day when we were alone together.

"First, I don't know. Second, he's rather a good chap."

"Eh? Rather a good chap? Man alive! I should have thought if any one would wish him to the devil it'd be you."

"Well, I don't. I like the chap," I rejoined, shortly.

Trask fired off a long whistle.

"That's good," he said. "That's good, coming from you of all people, Holt. Why he's cutting you out all along the line."

Then I fired off a speech.

"I won't pretend to misunderstand you, Trask," I said. "But that sort of remark is in the rottenest taste, in fact downright caddish. And look here. For a good while past you have laid yourself out to try and make me a butt for your stodgy wit. Well, I've had enough of that—more than enough. So chuck it. See? Chuck it."

"Oh, all right, Holt. Keep your hair on, old man. How beastly 'short' you've got in these days. You usen't to be."

There was an insinuation here conveyed that did not tend to soothe me, but possibly it was unintentional. Trask had a way of climbing down if tackled direct, that disarmed resentment. To do him justice, I don't think it was due to cowardice, but to a feeling that he had gone too far, and a natural shrinking on the part of a man not actually drunk or an idiot, from the possibility of being made to look foolish in a row of his own bringing on.

One wet and drizzling day George, who was riding round the place with me during one of my tours of inspection, burst forth with—

"Man, but that chap Pentridge is dead spoons on Beryl."

"What are you talking about?" I said, rather roughly, not relishing the topic, yet not unwilling, curiously enough, that he should pursue it.

"Why, of course he is. Any fool could see that. Why, they're always together, and then the way he looks, and the way he talks to her. I mean not what he says, but the way he says it. Of course they are spoons. But he's a fine chap—hey, Kenrick?"

The young rascal, it will be observed, had made a big brother of me by that time.

"That's a great yarn you've got hold of there, George," I answered, "but I should advise you not to be too fond of spinning it around, because I'm pretty certain Beryl wouldn't like it."

"Oh, of course I wouldn't say it to any one but you, Kenrick," he answered, rather hurt. I had taken the youngster somewhat under my wing of late, and he was keen to accompany me on my rounds. It had been decided that he must on no account be allowed to go about alone; in fact, his father had been advised to send him right away out of the locality altogether, and was even then negotiating for a school for him in Port Elizabeth or Cape Town. It could not be too far, it was represented.

The boy's inconsequent chatter had given another turn to the knife. He was a sharp youngster, and prone to get in everybody's way. Probably he had seen or heard more between the two than we had, but as to this, of course, I should curtly have shut him up had he volunteered any such narrative to me.

"We'll just look round by Jabavu's flock, and then go home," I said.

"*Ja*, let's. It's beastly cold, and I've had enough of it," he answered, as if that decided the matter.

Cold it assuredly was. A thin penetrating drizzle was falling, and the hilltops over beyond the valley were hidden in mist. Dotting the slope in front, which looked indescribably dreary in the drawing-in afternoon, a spread of white specks and patches represented a thousand or so of sheep.

"Why, there are several Kafirs there with Jabavu," said George. "Look, Kenrick. There are at least three of them—no, two—counting him."

The herd, as we drew near, made a great show of rounding up his flock. The other two stood still, awaiting our arrival. They gave me sullen greeting.

"What do you do here, you two? Who are you?" I said in Kafir, which I could talk fairly well by that time. And hardly had I uttered the words when I recognised the big savage, Sibuko, and in the other the fellow who had announced his amiable intention of cutting my throat up there in the cattle-stealers' cave. "You. What is your name?" I went on, pointing at this latter.

"Maqala."

The fellow was staring at me with an expression of impudent menace. I didn't relish his off-hand way of answering, and it was all I could do to restrain myself from laying my whip about his shoulders; but I remembered that we had had enough trouble of late, and it would be as well to avoid a fresh quarrel. So I said—

"Go, Maqala. Go, Sibuko. You have no business here. Go."

They muttered something as they slouched their blankets around them, and strolled leisurely away. But for one moment, as their glances rested on the boy, the expression of their countenances was such that I thought it would be well if those school negotiations could be brought to a head as soon as possible. Anyhow, that they were here to-day for no good was as certain as that they were here at all.

"I wonder if they've been 'slaag-ing,'" said George.

Evidently he was under no apprehension on the other head, which was as well.

"I don't think so," I answered, "but we can count and see." So we called Jabavu, and having halted our horses a little way apart, made him drive the whole flock slowly between us. The count was correct.

The herd, who was one of Kuliso's people, declared that these two had merely sat down for a while to have a chat. What harm could they do? he said. They were not even disturbing the game, for they had no dogs.

This was undeniable, but I had a very uncomfortable feeling on the subject of the encounter; and a conviction that these two scoundrels had joined hands through no mere chance, but were watching their opportunity for mischief, forced itself in upon my mind more and more; and as we rode home in the gathering dusk, I almost forgot my own troubles in thinking out what form such mischief might take, and how to guard against it.

A presentiment is a wholly arbitrary thing and subject to no laws of reasoning whatever. Such a presentiment was upon me then. I felt irresistibly that some danger hung over some or all of us, and that when we should be least on our guard. Well, the only way to defeat it was never to be off our guard.

Chapter Twenty Five.

Dumela's defection.

"What do you think of this, Kenrick?" said Brian, as I went into the cattle kraal at milking time a couple of mornings after. "Here's old Dumela saying he wants to leave."

The old cattle-herd was squatted on his heels on the ground. Brian and his father were seated on a log listening to what he had to say. This was not much. His brother's son had got into trouble at Gangelizwe's "Great Place," away beyond the Tsomo, and had involved his brother too. He must go and help them at once, taking with him the several head of cattle he had running on the farm. He was getting old, and thought he would not work any more.

"Why, he's been with you close on twenty years, hasn't he?" I said.

"Rather more," answered Brian. "But that's always the way with these chaps. The longer they've been with you the more keen they are on clearing out for a change: for I don't swallow over-much of that brother's son yarn. Well, he'll have to go, I suppose—eh, dad?"

"Oh, yes." Then it was put to Dumela that he was behaving shabbily in taking himself off at a moment's notice after all these years, and that, too, just at a time when we were in need of a thoroughly trustworthy man to fill his position, after our friction with Kuliso. This he deprecatorily admitted. Still, if his relatives stood in need of him, what else could he do? And he was not leaving us entirely in the lurch, for he had found a man who was ready to take his place now at once, and who was a good man with cattle. In fact, he was over in his hut now.

"Well, we'd better see him, at any rate," said Brian, and calling one of the boys, despatched him to Dumela's hut to fetch the stranger. The boy reappeared in no time followed by—Maqala.

This fellow saluted us gravely, but showed no sign of ever having seen any of us before. I own his sudden appearance startled me. Was this part of the game, I wondered, and if so how on earth could it be that an old and faithful servant like Dumela could aid and abet any mischief that might be brewing against us? Yet having good reason to bear in mind this rascal's excellent knowledge of English, I could utter no word of warning. It was, however, unnecessary, for Brian had recognised him at once as the man I had pointed out in the street at Fort Lamport.

"Why, that is one of Kuliso's people," he said. "You are a Tembu, Dumela; how then can you bring me a man of another tribe, and vouch for him as good?"

Dumela's reply to this seemed lame, and deepened my suspicions more and more. Would it be well, I wondered, to engage Maqala, and thus have him more under our own observation? But Septimus Matterson cut the knot of the difficulty.

"I won't have him," he said. "I won't have him at any price. I've seen him before, and I don't want to see him again. He is one of the people who raided us that day, one of the foremost of them too. I wouldn't trust him further than I could see him, so he may take himself off."

There was no getting round the straight directness of this reply. Maqala said nothing. He just flung his blanket round him, and lounged away; but as he did so the look he turned on me was not a pleasant one. On *me*. I was conscious of a feeling of relief. I, then, was the object of his hostility. Whatever nefarious scheme he was hatching, I was the destined victim of it—I and not the boy. Well, that simplified the situation, for I was flattered to think I knew how to take care of myself. Yet, even then his implacability was not quite comprehensible, for Kafirs, as a rule, have a strong sense of justice and are not vindictive when they realise that they have deserved whatever punishment they may have got, and if this one did not deserve the somewhat rough treatment I had twice meted out to him, why I didn't know who did. Physically he was a tall, lithe specimen of his race, rather light-coloured, and had an evil cast of countenance. The expression of that countenance now, as he darted that quick parting glance at me, reminded me of nothing so much as a roused snake.

Well, Dumela took himself off. He made no profuse apologies or extravagant expressions on the strength of thus terminating his twenty years' service. He just bade us farewell, collected his two wives, his cattle, and such pay as was due to him, and went. We had to put on one of our farm boys in his place, and were to that extent short-handed, necessitating more general supervision, which, as Brian was obliged to be away from home on a matter of business, considerably tended to enlarge my own sphere of energy. But for this I was not sorry, as it took me more and more away from the house.

Sometimes Pentridge would accompany me on my rides abroad, and I was glad to have him, for he was always good company, and, liking the man for his own sake, I could not feel mean enough to hate him for being more fortunate than myself. On one such occasion—Beryl having laughingly but firmly ordered him out of the schoolroom where she was giving Iris, and now George, their morning lessons, and thus throwing him for refuge on me—he said something that set me thinking.

"D'you know, Holt, I'm beginning to feel beastly jealous of you."

"So? And why?"

"Why, the way you seem to have captured every one here."

"Didn't know it."

"But you have. Why, it's 'Holt says this' and 'Kenrick thinks that' on all hands, till I believe if you weren't such a good chap I'd rather dislike you."

"'You do me proud,' Pentridge—unless, that is, you're pulling my leg. Otherwise I hadn't the faintest idea of anything of the kind, and don't see why it should be so now."

I believe I spoke with needless bitterness, but at the moment I could not help thinking how much greater reason I had for disliking him.

"Well, but it is. Good old Matterson isn't effusive, as you know, and I've never heard him boom any one before. But he's always booming you. That time the Kafirs made that raid on you, he swears you stood by him like a brick."

"Well, I could hardly turn tail and run away, could I?"

"Not only that, but he said he was astonished at the judgment you showed on the occasion. And only this morning he was thanking his stars you were so good at bossing up things, now that he was seedy, and rheumatic, and Brian had to be away a lot."

Here was some practical cause for self-satisfaction, I thought. In view of my utter ruin financially, it was gratifying to know that I was deemed worth my salt in any one line of livelihood. But I answered—

"Well, if you've put your hand to the plough it's satisfactory to know that you're driving a straight furrow."

"Rather. Brian, too, is always booming you, and as for those two kids, why they don't cheek you a bit."

"Is that a sign of esteem?" I laughed, for the idea tickled me. Further, I admit a littleness—in the shape of an anxiety to hear whether Beryl had added her quota to the general testimonial, and if so on what terms. But, by accident or design, he forebore to gratify me.

"I should say so," he rejoined. "Knowing their natural temperaments, it means that they must hold you in profound respect—especially George."

"Poor little devil! He's had the cheek considerably taken out of him of late," I said. "He used to be rather an outrage."

"So I should imagine. By the way, Holt, they were telling me about how you got Iris out of the sea that time at East London. It was—"

But whatever "it was" I didn't want to hear.

"Stop there, Pentridge," I said. "That's a forbidden topic and one I'm completely sick of. It was mere child's play to a fellow who is as thoroughly at home in the water as I am, so don't talk about it."

"Oh, all right, old chap," he answered good-humouredly, and then he went on to tell me something about himself. He had been some years in a slow Dutch township on the border line between the Eastern and Western Province, and had come to Fort Lamport to try and set up a practice there if he could buy out the District Surgeon, who was old and inclined to be shaky. "Yes," I thought somewhat bitterly, "and his reasons for coming to that particular place are not difficult to fathom."

For it was obvious to my mind that things were coming to a head. He and Beryl were a great deal together, and more and more of an excellent understanding seemed to exist between them, and in the light of this it seemed equally obvious that, apart from the catastrophe which had overtaken myself, I had been indulging in false hopes before—living in a fool's paradise, and I don't know whether the discovery rendered the situation any better for me or not.

One day I came upon them out riding. I had been doing an exhaustive round of the place and struck the main road. The bush grew right down to this on each side, and as I gained it I could see two other riders approaching. Even then I would have withdrawn, not wishing to be the one too many, but they had seen me. Yet I had seen them a little before: had seen how happy they looked together, and, with a jealous pang, how well they looked together, how completely they seemed to match.

Beryl was looking lovely, the warm paleness of her face just suffused by the exercise, and the generous kiss of the free open air with just a sparkle of crisp keenness in it. She looked splendid in the saddle, too, as she always did, sitting her horse with the most perfect ease and grace—Meerkat, that very horse I had risked my life to recover and restore to her. Many a similar ride had we had together, she and I. And ah! how little I had appreciated it then, I found myself thinking; yet now to look back upon those times! But they would not bear looking back upon.

Pentridge seemed, I thought, ever so slightly put out as I joined them, yet he need not have, for whatever my failings I flattered myself I was not quite such a fool as Trask, and consequently knew when I was not wanted. Beryl, on the other hand, did not give even the most subtle indication of disturbance; but then, after all, women are much better actors than we are.

"Had a good ride?" I asked carelessly, dropping the bridle rein on the horse's neck, and shielding a match with my hands to light a pipe.

"Er—yes. Jolly," answered Pentridge. But Beryl said—

"I don't think there's much chance of anything going wrong on the place while you're about, Kenrick. Why, you're as good as ten policemen."

"Don't know if that's to be taken as a compliment after the way I've heard some of you talk of that useful force," I answered with a laugh.

"Why, of course it is. But you are really too good about it. You might take it easy now and then."

"Oh, that's all right," I rejoined in would-be airy tone. "Best thing in the world for me. I enjoy it."

Beryl's large eyes, deep with one of those strange, unfathomable glances in which she sometimes indulged, were full on my face. I fancied Pentridge was making an effort not to fidget uneasily. Well, I was not going to be a marplot; and flattered myself there was nothing of the dog-in-the-manger about me, as I replied—

"Well, I shall have to leave you now. By the time I get to the vee-kraal it will be counting-in time. And the oftener Notuba's sheep are counted, the better, in my opinion."

I fancied that Pentridge's face cleared, for he knew that the course I now proposed to pursue would take me away at right angles from their line of march, viz. the main road. But the same did not hold good of Beryl.

"I thought you were going to ride home with us," she said; and if the tone was not one of genuine disappointment, why then she was even a better actress than I had at first reckoned her.

"I wish I could," I answered. "But now Brian's away, you know! You see it's a matter I take a pride in."

"Yes, I know you do," she said; and there was that in her way of saying it that brought back all the old time.

"Well then, 'duty calls,'" I rejoined, forcing a laugh. "So long. We shall meet again in the vast length of an hour or so."

As I turned my horse and struck into the bush path I prided myself on my own acting powers. In point of fact, I had no intention of going to the vee-kraal—none whatever. There was no necessity to, seeing I had counted out there that same morning and had found the count correct. But 'two's company, three's a crowd' if a threadbare, is eke a wholesome axiom, and I did not choose, under the circumstances, to constitute the crowd. But it was time I broke off from them if I wanted to keep up my rôle; yet I could not help speculating as to what had transpired during that ride. Had anything? From their looks as I joined them, it might have. Or from Pentridge's look when I branched off, it might yet be to come. But then in that case, why did

Beryl so genuinely wish me to accompany them the rest of the way? Well, well. Time would show.

Chapter Twenty Six.

Opportunity?

"By the way, what have I done to you, Kenrick?"

We were walking together, Beryl and I, in the garden, just as we had walked on the evening of my arrival, only that now the shade had nearly vanished with the fall of leaves. We had not walked together thus alone since prior to the tragedy, but to-day it happened that Pentridge was out with Septimus Matterson, and as I had mentioned an intention of doing something to the garden, Beryl had joined me. We had walked on thus together, chatting about the piece of work I had in hand, when she suddenly faced round on me with the above query.

"Done to me?" I echoed rather blankly. "Done to me? What do you mean, Beryl?"

"Well, why have you avoided me so of late—rather markedly, too?"

Rather markedly? Great heaven! And here I had been priding myself all this while upon having played my part so well, above all so unobtrusively. And this was what it had amounted to—that I had avoided her "rather markedly." But there was no trace of resentment, of temper, in her tone. It was merely that of one desiring information, and her great eyes were bent straight and searchingly upon my face.

What was I to say? I became conscious that I was staring stupidly at her, but if only she could have read my mind! Yet I could hardly read it myself. All sorts of whirling confused thoughts were chasing each other through it, as I looked at her standing there, sweet, and cool, and graceful, and wholly alluring, but—not for me, ah no! not for me. How could I tell her of the bitter upheaval of the last couple of weeks? How could I tell her the truth without telling her the whole truth? How could I tell her that I, a beggared pauper, had been striving to stifle and live down the love I had been on the point of declaring? It was too late for that, and, over and above, would not such a declaration now be simply a cheapening of myself; now that I had assured myself that, in any event, whatever love she had to give was not for me? What was I to say? I could not deny that I had avoided her. Her natural quick-wittedness and woman's instinct were not to be set aside in any so light a fashion, yet I shrank from laying my own wounds bare.

"Why, don't you see what a lot I've had to do, Beryl?" I said. "Rather more than usual of late. And you've had a visitor to entertain, too. Pentridge is a good chap, isn't he?"

All this I rattled out airily, and in the most natural manner in the world, as I thought. But she was not taken in.

"You haven't been yourself at all for some time, Kenrick," she went on, "not since we came back, anyhow. I'm not the only one who has noticed it."

"So? Who else has?" I asked laughingly.

"Well, Dr Pentridge for one. We were talking about you the other day, and he said you gave him the idea of a man who had something on his mind. He's a doctor, you see."

"Ho-ho! Quite so; and now he's trying to capture a fee out of consulting hours," I laughed. "Never mind, Beryl. We won't call in Pentridge professionally just yet."

I had a spade in my hand, and with it I set to work to clear away a slight obstruction in the furrow beneath the quince hedge; and while I did so I realised that my laugh did not ring true, that it no more imposed upon Beryl than it did upon myself.

"By the way," I went on, "he's coming to practice in Fort Lamport, he tells me. That'll be handy if I want to put him in charge of my case."

"Kenrick, will you stop joking and be serious," she said. "First of all, answer my first question. Have I done or said anything to offend you?"

"Why, good heavens! of course not. How on earth could you?"

"That's a weight off my mind, at any rate," she answered with a little smile.

I stood and faced her.

"Look here, Beryl," I said. "To prevent any misunderstanding I'll tell you this much. I have something on my mind just now, but it relates to matters of business. I had some rather nasty news from England the day before you came back, and it has worried me a good bit. That's all."

But she shook her head.

"I doubt if that is all," she said, and my pulses were set a-hammering as I wondered whether she was going to get the rest of it out of me too. "I believe it is worse than you are admitting. I don't want to pry into your affairs, Kenrick, but you are like one of ourselves now, and I can't bear to see you going about looking as you have been doing of late. And—and—you might do worse than consult father or Brian about it. They are both very shrewd in that line you know, and might be of use to you."

"Well, it may come to that," I answered. "But meanwhile, Beryl, what I have told you is between ourselves. You made me tell you, you know. Heaven knows I never intended to whine to you about my sordid grievances."

"Kenrick, don't," she said, impulsively putting forth her hand to rest on mine. "'Whine,' indeed! That isn't you anyway. Why, I am proud of your confidence, and sorry—oh, so sorry—for its cause. But you must cheer up. I have an instinct that everything will come right. It sometimes does, you know."

Would it? I thought I knew better, but I had done enough grizzling already, so was not going to say so. And I thought with a certain bitterness that her sympathy, sweet as it was, was not of the nature I could have wished it to be. Even then the concern in her tone, the softening of her eyes, the touch of her hand as she stood facing me, scattered my resolution to the winds. She should know all, then and there—all—all.

"So you think that everything will come right, do you?" I said, pretending to do something with the spade so as not to be obliged to look at her.

"Yes. I have an instinct that way."

"But if it can't?"

"That is an 'if' in which my belief is somewhat feeble," she answered confidently.

"Supposing I—er, supposing a man had lost all he had in the world, and that beyond all possibility of recovery—what then?"

"He might remedy the loss. Energy, some resourcefulness, and a great deal of common sense, constitute not a bad foundation for a fresh start—say in a country like this."

The cool, practical, matter-of-fact tone of this reply fairly startled me—and then—Great Scott! the remarks that Pentridge had let fall during our conversation a day or two back, gratifying to myself in that they reflected the estimation in which I seemed to be held, flashed across my mind. Beryl's words were spoken with a purpose—were meant to be taken home, and with the idea came another. Could I, without anything definite passing between us, turn the key of her mind as regarded herself?

"Yes, he might remedy the loss—after a time," I said, still pretending to work with the spade—still not looking at her. "After a time. But what if that time were too late?"

"Could it ever be?"

"Why, yes. Because by that time what would have made success worth striving for might be no longer attainable; might have passed out of reach irrevocably and for ever."

She did not answer. In the tensity of the silence the clink of my spade in the dry dusty furrow seemed to my wrought-up mind to sound as with a loud hammering. A network of sunlight, from the deep blue of an early winter sky, fell through the nearly denuded boughs upon the earth around, and the screech of crickets and the far-off melodious shout of a hoepoe hardly seemed to break the stillness. What would she answer? Or would she even understand? And as to this I almost hoped not, for here had I, under cover of this veiled talk, been saying to her in effect: "Beryl, I am a ruined man, a beggar, but—how would it be to throw away the best years of your life and wait for me on the off chance of my ever being able to rise substantially above that most unenviable position?"

"Of course I am only putting a case," I appended with conscious lameness.

"Oh, of course," she answered readily. "But, supposing—"

"Beryl! Beryl!" rang out a clear, child-voice, *crescendo*. "Oh, there you are. I thought she had gone to the garden, Dr Pentridge," this last back over a shoulder, and Iris came tearing along the path, tossing back the wealth of her gold-brown hair. After her, in more leisurely fashion, came Pentridge.

He started on seeing me, so plainly, so unmistakably, that, keenly observant, I at once set up the theory within my own mind that he had come to find Beryl alone, with a purpose of course. The child could easily have been got rid of, but I—well, that was a different matter.

"Ha, Holt! Hard at it as usual?" he said, with rather a forced geniality.

"Not particularly hard. Only filling up an odd moment."

He told us that he had just received letters by a messenger who had ridden out from Fort Lamport, letters relating to his pending negotiations, which would render it necessary for him to leave as soon as possible; in fact, that very afternoon if it could possibly be managed. He would have to go straight home from there, so supposed it would be a final good-bye, though we should all meet again soon—in fact, quite soon, he hoped.

I don't know whether I did, and that for obvious reasons. However, it was manifest that he wanted to have a talk with Beryl, and he should have it, so far as I was concerned; to which end I started in on a battle of chaff with Iris, which kept her busy for a few minutes, then craftily manoeuvred her further down the kloof to look at and talk over a couple of bees' nests we had been planning to take out. This was all right enough, but what does the little fiend do next but splutter out—

"Can you keep a secret, Kenrick? Because if so I'll tell you one. Pentridge is awfully smashed on Beryl."

"I should say *Dr* Pentridge if I was a little girl," I formulated to the accompaniment of rather a ghastly grin. "Well, is that the secret? because if so I haven't said I could keep one yet."

"*Ach*! Well, you won't say I said so, hey?"

"I won't say anything at all about it, Iris," I answered magisterially. "And little girls oughtn't to think about such things."

She opened her big blue eyes wide at the reproof. Then detecting the mirth—such as it was—depicted on my own face, she bestowed such a whole-souled pinch upon my brown and bared forearm, as caused me to sing out and stamp.

"You spiteful little cat. Wait till we get at those bees' nests. You deserve to be jolly well stung."

She pranced round me, chuckling maliciously.

"Ha-ha! That's what you get for coming the solemn old school-baas over me," she crowed. Then—"There, there. You're not *kwaat* with me, are you?"

The insinuating little rogue. As if she didn't know she could have done anything she liked to me!

We did not take out the bees' nests that day. My mind was full of what had gone before, and I listened to the sunny child's chatter, fearful lest her precocious eyes should see through my own secret—wondering, too, whether her interruption of us had been for good or the reverse. She had interrupted us at a critical juncture. What had Beryl been on the point of saying to me? What was she saying even then to that other? Had I let slip an opportunity? And yet—and yet I if so, how could I have seized such opportunity under the circumstances? Of course I could not.

But what she had or had not said to that other seemed likely to remain a mystery, and the same held good of what he had said to her, for neither by word or hint did Beryl let fall any inkling of the matter.

After Pentridge had gone, things seemed to shake down as usual, but for me a line was drawn, and the glowing, idyllic happiness of the last few months seemed shut back as though beyond an iron door.

One day when Septimus Matterson and I were alone together, something moved me to follow Beryl's advice and tell him of my disaster—though I had hardly done so than I felt it was a more complete burning of my boats. He was very concerned, and said so.

"Don't lose heart, though, Kenrick," he said. "Many a man has had a bigger knock than that and has come out smiling. When do you say you will know beyond all doubt whether things are—as bad as you think?"

"Oh, in a month or two."

"Well, we'll talk over it again then. But—don't lose heart. And remember this, Kenrick. You are as one of ourselves now, and if the worst comes to the worst, this place is always your home as long as you like to make it so."

I mumbled out something that was meant to be appreciative, and then he began to talk about other things. He was rather put out because his plans on George's account had fallen through. The schools he had been negotiating with delicately but firmly refused to take the boy.

"I'm coming round to the conclusion that there's no necessity to send him away at all," he ended up. "The thing has been settled and is now a thing of the past. I believe he's as safe as you or I."

To this what answer could I make, remembering that the speaker was nothing if not a man of sound judgment? Yet even the soundest of such may fall into an error—and then!

Chapter Twenty Seven.

"There were two Lives."

"They are late—very late. They ought to be here by now," murmured Beryl, more to herself than to me, as she came out on the stoep, where I was seated alone, admiring the splendid moonlight; "they" being her father and George, who had ridden over to Trask's early in the afternoon about something, intending to be home by supper-time. Now it was nearly bedtime, and still there was no sign of them.

"Oh, they'll turn up any minute now," I said. "It's not likely they'll stay the night at Trask's, I suppose?"

"Not in the least likely. But—I wish they'd come."

Brian was away, Iris too; the latter staying with some people at Fort Lamport—so that Beryl and I were alone together. But as she dropped into one of the roomy cane chairs beside me, I could see that she had hardly an ear for half my conversation, and her face, clearly visible in the moonlight, wore a strangely anxious and troubled look. The slightest sound would start her up, listening intently. I watched her with amazement.

"Why, Beryl," I said. "What on earth is the reason of all this anxiety? They—all of us—have been out as late as this before?"

"And I have never been as anxious as this before. Quite true. But, do you believe in instincts, in presentiments, Kenrick?"

"Well, in a way perhaps. But—I hardly know. They are generally to be traced to overwrought nerves, and that's a complaint I should have thought would be the last for you to suffer from, Beryl."

"Yes, it seems strange. All the more reason why my instinct in this case is a true one. I feel as if something terrible was about to happen—was happening—and I—we—can do nothing—nothing. Oh, I can't sit still."

She rose and paced the stoep up and down, then descended the steps and stood looking out into the night. This sort of thing is catching. And that Beryl, the courageous, the clear-headed, the strong-nerved, should be thus thrown off her balance, was inexplicable, more than mysterious. Something of a cold creep seemed to steal over my own nerves. The night was strangely still; warm too for the time of year, by rights it ought to have been sharp and frosty. Even the intermittent voices of nocturnal bird or insect were hushed, but every now and then the silence would be broken by the dismal moaning and stamping of a herd of cattle gathered round the slaughter place behind the waggon shed. But these impressions promptly gave way to the love which welled up within me a hundredfold as I gazed into the sweet troubled eyes, for I had joined her where she stood in front of the stoep.

"Dearest, don't give way to these imaginings," I urged. "They will grow upon you till you make yourself quite ill. What can there be to fear? Nothing."

Great heavens! my secret was out. What had I said? And—how would Beryl take it?

The latter I was not destined to learn—at any rate not then. The dogs, which had been lying behind the house, uttering an occasional sleepy growl when the moaning, scuffling cattle became too noisy, now leaped up and charged wildly forward, uttering such a clamour as to have been heard for miles.

"Here they are, you see. I told you they'd be home directly," I said. "And here they are."

But the intense relief which momentarily had lighted up Beryl's face faded, giving way to a look of deepened anxiety and disappointment.

"It is not them at all," she murmured. "Listen!"

By the sound of their barking, the dogs must have gained the further gate. The clamour had ceased—suddenly, mysteriously. Yet, listening intently, we could detect no sound of voices nor yet of hoof strokes, both of which would have been audible a mile or more away in the calm stillness of the night. Yet, from an occasional "woof" or so, which they could not restrain, we could hear that the dogs were returning.

But their tumult broke forth again, though partially and momentarily. Someone was opening the inner gate.

An exclamation escaped Beryl, low, but intense. A dark figure came towards us.

"Why, it is Dumela!" she gasped.

"*Inkosikazi*," began the old Kafir, whom we all thought considerably more than a hundred miles away at that moment, if we had thought of him at all, that is. "*Inkosikazi*. Where is your father? I would speak with him, now at once."

"He is not here, Dumela. He will be, any moment, though."

"*Au*! I thought not. I thought not," was the muttered answer. "And Jojo (George)?"

"He is with his father," said Beryl eagerly. "Why?"

The old man muttered something quickly to himself. Then aloud—

"They have not returned? That is well. *Inkosikazi*, take horse, and go and tell them the way home is dark to-night—dark, dark. Let them sleep where they are, and return beneath the sun."

"Dark?" I interrupted, like an idiot. "Dark? Why it's nearly full moon."

Dumela glanced at me impatiently, eke somewhat contemptuously.

"*Au*!" he said. "I have not been away for nothing. Why did I leave here? Why did I fill up the ears of my father with a tale? Why did I take away my cattle and my wives? Because the ears of Kuliso are large"—meaning open—"but I wanted mine to be so, too. So I went no further than the further border of Kuliso's location, giving out that I had a grievance against my father, whose milk and corn I had eaten for nearly the half of my lifetime; giving out, too, that I wanted it not to be known to those I had left, that I was dwelling beneath the shadow of Kuliso. Then the people of Kuliso feared not to talk within my hearing. Say, *Inkosikazi*, why has not your father—and mine—sent the boy away?"

Beryl's face went ghastly white.

"Why, Dumela," she said. "The compensation cattle have been paid, and Kuliso has assured us the unfortunate affair was settled. He is the chief. We have his word."

"You have his word. But the fathers of the children have not the compensation cattle—no, not any of them. Kuliso's hands are large. That which is poured into them does not overflow and fall out. The fathers of the children who were killed have no compensation, and—the boy was not punished. Justice—the white man's justice—has not been done, they say. Why was he still kept here?"

Beryl's face seemed cut out of stone. She made a step towards the old Kafir, and placed a hand on each shoulder. They were about the same height, and I saw her grasp tighten, on him, like a vice.

"Attend, Dumela. Are they in danger now, and where? Quick, do you hear? Quick."

"Take the shortest way to the house of the Chatterer (Trask)," he answered, thus directly cornered. "*Au*! were there not two lives taken, two lives! And these are two lives."

Almost flinging him from her, Beryl turned to me, and in her face, her tone, her gesture, was a very whirlwind of apprehension, of frenzied despair.

"Kenrick, what horses are in the stable?"

"Fortunately two—yours, Meerkat—and mine."

"Saddle them up, quick. Get your revolver, and come."

Not long did it take me to obey her behest, and indeed, no sooner had I done so than Beryl herself appeared at the stable door, equipped for our expedition.

Giving no further thought to old Dumela, we fared forth over the moonlit veldt.

"My presentiment was a true one after all, Kenrick," remarked Beryl, as we rode side by side.

"That remains to be seen," I said. "Old Dumela may have found a mare's nest."

"No. He would not have come here at this time of night like this without good reason. And all the time we were thanking him shabby and ungrateful he was serving us—watching over our interests, our safety."

The short cut to Trask's lay along the bottom of a network of intersecting kloofs, but the path would only allow of riding single file. Beryl and I had a sharp skirmish as to who should take the lead, but I claimed my right, and firmly stuck to it. If there was danger, mine was the right to discover it and meet it first, and that she recognised.

Heavens! the sickening, creeping mystery of that night ride—the weird, boding awe of it, as we took our way through the dark gloom of overhanging scrub, the sharp contrast of its blackness with the vivid glare of the full moon accentuated tenfold—the ghostly cliffs frowning down upon us, as from a scene in Dante.

Our way took us by the lower end of the Zwaart Kloof, the site of that other tragedy—the scene, too, of my fell and fatal discovery when all my castles in the air had melted away, when I had learned that I was ruined, and as we entered its bushy recesses a thrill of superstitious dread ran through me. It was an ill-omened spot—cursed and haunted with an overshadowing of woe. Surely—surely—not again were its shades destined to cover another tragedy—another outpouring of the cup of horror and of evil.

I had but lately avowed my disbelief in instincts, yet here I know not what instinct of dread and repulsion came upon me as we drew near the place, moving me to glance over my shoulder to catch a glimpse of the face of my companion, possibly with the intent to ascertain whether the same idea was moving her. But as I did so a sudden and violent start on the part of my horse came near unseating me. Shying, snorting, the brute swerved and backed; and coming thus into collision with Beryl's steed it took both of us some moments to soothe and quiet the animals. But in that brief flash of time I had caught a glimpse of a Something lying on the ground, and my heart stood still within me and every drop of blood in my system seemed to turn to water.

There was no mistaking the nature of that Something. The inanimate human form is possessed of an eloquence all its own. Dark upon the shimmer of the moonlit earth this one lay, the white face staring upward to the sky, the face of poor little George Matterson. And the same instinctive conviction flashed through us both as we slid from our saddles, that it was a dead face.

Never, if I were to live a thousand years, could I forget the whirl of rage and horror and grief that convulsed me at that moment, turning me half-dazed. Beryl was beside the prostrate form, bending over it. No cry had escaped her, only a quick, half-stifled gasp. In a moment I was beside her, having taken the precaution to secure both our horses.

"Dead!" she uttered, having raised the head, with infinite tenderness of touch. "Dead. Murdered!"

I don't know which feeling was uppermost within my mind at that moment— horror at the discovery, or awe of the strange, unnatural calmness wherewith she accepted the frightful and heartrending situation. I bent down over the poor remains. A noosed *reim* had been twisted round the neck, compressing it tightly. Not this, however, had been the cause of death. The grass around and beneath the body glistened with a dark wet stain. On the dead boy's clothing above the heart was a clean cut from which blood was still welling. He had been stabbed—stabbed with an assegai.

We stood staring into each other's faces, ashy white in the moonlight. It seemed as if our lips refused to frame the question that was in both our minds. Then, speaking in a harsh, gasping whisper, Beryl said—

"What of—father?"

Chapter Twenty Eight.

"Walk, Kuliso!"

"Two lives were taken, and these are two lives."

The words of old Dumela were humming through my brain, as I bent over the dead boy in quest of spoor. Such was plain and abundant, and showed that he had not been slain here, but had been deposited after death on the spot where we had found him. But that we should find Septimus Matterson alive neither of us ever for a moment dared to hope.

There was no difficulty in following the spoor by that clear light. The savage murderers had left quite a broad path where they had dragged their victim. No word did we exchange, Beryl and I. It was significant that no thought of personal danger was in our minds, only a sickening apprehension of what we were, at any moment, likely to come upon, mingled with a fierce longing for revenge by reason of what we had already found. These midnight assassins might even now be lying in wait for us. Every bush might shelter a lurking foe, yet for our own safety we had no thought. More than once in the course of my experiences I have found myself in peril of my own life, but my feelings on such occasions have been nothing to the awful boding suspense of that search, through the still, unearthly midnight silence.

Suddenly our horses, which we had been leading as we followed the spoor, snorted, and rucked back, nearly wrenching the bridles from our grasp. Instinctively we both drew our revolvers; instinctively, too, we knew that it was not the living that had startled the animals, but the dead.

Our quest was at an end. Septimus Matterson lay in full view, there in the clear moonlight, but even before Beryl had rushed forward and thrown herself beside him, we knew that there was no more life here than in the poor little remains we had just left at no great distance away.

Yet, what had slain him? The attitude was calm and peaceful, for he lay on his side as though asleep. No trace of wound or blow was upon him, whereas the body of poor little George showed every mark of brutal violence, from the deadly stab to the agonised contortion of his face. But Septimus Matterson's strong, fine features were placid and undisfigured. Then I remembered what Beryl had told me about her father's life.

"He has not been killed," I whispered. "His heart has failed."

She nodded, but did not speak; and at that moment I could piece together the whole of this grisly tragedy which the silent midnight bush had witnessed: the fell carrying out of this grim vendetta which we ought all to have known about and guarded against before it was too late. The two had been waylaid and set upon suddenly when returning from Trask's, and while George had been the main object of the vengeance of the murderers the sudden shock of the surprise had stricken his father dead through heart failure. That the body of the latter had suffered no violence after death might have been due to the respect in which he had been held while living, whereas the noosed ram which had been placed around the neck of the boy seemed to add a lurid significance to old Dumela's words, "'*Justice—the white man's justice—has not been done,' they say.*"

Beryl's expression of countenance was unfathomable, as she knelt there supporting her dead father's head, tenderly stroking back the hair from the forehead, wiping the cold, marble face with her white handkerchief. And I, as I stood there gazing down upon the man who had been to me as a father and a friend, and knew that we should never again hear his voice, never again see those kindly eyes light up with mirth or recognition, that his presence was removed from our midst for ever, I believe I should have broken down and burst out blubbering like a schoolboy but for what next occurred.

Beryl, having gently lowered the inanimate head, now rose. But no tears glistened in her eyes. They were dry and hard with the terrible intensity of the strain. No cry, no burst of agony escaped her breast; but as she stood there, her tall form drawn to its full height, the look upon her face was so awful, so blasting in its fury of hate and despair and menace, that even in that moment of grief and horror I almost recoiled from her. Heavens! Had her grief in its reaction merged itself into this intensity, this overmastering impulse of hate and revenge? If so, it seemed that her brain must give way.

"Come," she said, moving to the side of her horse.

"But, can you leave him—them?" I urged.

Was it a laugh—blood-curdling, maniacal—or was it the snarl of a bereaved wild beast?

"We can leave them—now," she said. "First—justice. The justice of revenge. Come."

Gaining her saddle without my aid she led the way from that evil and accursed spot. But it was the opposite way to that by which we had come. She uttered no word. But the positions were reversed now. She led, and I followed—wondering.

We reached the high ridge at the head of the kloof, then descended into the valley wherein, much higher up, the house stood. This we left, and, crossing the valley, ascended by a steep track to a high "neck" which cleft the heights on the further side. We had by this time been riding for nearly an hour.

Now, as we halted to breathe our horses, and sat in our saddles, gazing forth upon the more open country beyond, before us the shadowy veldt, stretching away into moonlit dimness, was lit up here and there in the distance by twinkling points of light, over which hung a misty glow. These were the fires in the Ndhlambe location, whence, ever and again, in humming waves of sound, came a weird rhythmical chant, to a strange stamping accompaniment, varied by the howling of dogs or the faint shrill laughter of women. The savages were enjoying themselves in uproarious merrymaking.

No word had Beryl uttered all this time, but now she spoke, and the words which she did say fairly startled me, for they were of such import that I knew the chances were as fifty to one against either or both of us living to see the light of another day. She read off my thoughts as in a flash.

"Do not let me take you into this, Kenrick. After all, there is a risk. I can bring it off alone."

"Do be just to me, dear," I said gently, putting forth my hand till it rested on hers. "Do you think the idea of deserting you ever crossed my mind for the single fraction of an instant? It was of you I was thinking. Now listen. Leave this to me. I will do exactly what you have been planning—I alone. I will carry it out to the letter. Life is nothing to me—forgive me for speaking selfishly at such a time. Go back to—to them. I pledge you my word of honour and my life that I will do all you would have done. But you?—you must not embark in such an undertaking as this. Now—will you leave it to me?"

"No—a thousand times no. Kenrick, you are loyal and brave as few men are. Pardon my doubting you, or seeming to, for I never did so really."

In spite of the grief and woe which had come upon us, of the desperate undertaking to which we were pledged, a thrill of genuine exaltation set my pulses tingling at her words, her tone. We were close together. Our horses, glad of even this temporary rest, were standing still. I was going into almost certain death—with her, and I would not have exchanged the situation for any other on earth. A wild, well-nigh uncontrollable impulse seized me. Her great eyes were turned full upon mine, and the pallid hardness of her face seemed to relax. Then the recollection of what had happened, of what we had just looked upon, came back and I mastered the impulse. Assuredly if there was a time for all things this was not a time for some things—yet I read a meaning into a strange weary sigh that escaped her, as she gave the word to resume our way.

The Ndhlambe huts, beehive-shaped, yellow-thatched, lay clustering in the moonlight, spreading over the veldt far and wide. Innumerable they seemed, and from the dark, mimosa-stockaded enclosures came now and then a bleat, or the trumpet-like sneeze of a goat, and the sweet night air was unfragrant with the mingled odour of kine and wood smoke, and the musty reek of ochre-smeared Kafir humanity.

Most of the merrymakers had departed to their own kraals, but here and there, in that of the chief, dark groups still stood around. These gazed, with muttered wonder, upon this strange apparition of two white people riding into their midst at such a time of night, and one of those whites a woman. Formidable, too, they looked, those astonished and staring savages, many of them tall, well-nigh gigantic of frame, and you could see the rolling white of their distended eyeballs as they stood and gazed.

"Where is Kuliso? Where is the chief?"

The tone was firm, clear, audible to all. The Kafirs looked at each other.

"*Au*! That is his house, *Umlungase*," (white woman) and the speaker pointed to a large hut standing among a group. "But—it is night."

"Request him to come forth. I would talk with him," went on Beryl, speaking fluently in the vernacular, of which I, as I have before mentioned, had by this time picked up a very fair knowledge.

There was hesitation, muttered dissatisfaction, among the men, as we turned and headed straight for the hut they had pointed out, they following a short distance behind. The chief did not care to see visitors at such a time, was the not unnatural burden of their objections.

But just then two Kafirs emerged from one of the huts, and stood in front of us. One of them I recognised, and even were it otherwise the murmur of astonishment and profound deference which greeted his appearance would have been sufficient to identify him. The tall, fine form, the strong, bearded face, the lofty forehead with its air of command, I was not likely to forget. Now the expression of that face was divided between wonder and a scowl of resentment. Then Beryl spoke.

"I see you, Kuliso. What is the news, Kuliso?"

"*Whau*!" cried the chief, bringing his hand to his mouth in displeased amazement. "What is this? What does it mean?"

"This," said Beryl, covering him with her revolver. "Walk, Kuliso. Walk in front of me."

Then indeed the chief's exclamation of amazement was emphatic, and was echoed by those gathered around. A command—addressed to him! To *him*— and by a woman! But that unerring revolver covered him, and the skill of this particular woman was known to him—was known to most of those present.

There was no escape; and again that word—this time shorter and more crisp—

"Walk, Kuliso!"

The chief stared—stared at the deadly weapon—stared at the face behind it. Then he—walked.

I, too, looked at that face. The large eyes shone from its hard, deadly whiteness, with a fell and appalling stare. Could this be the face whose sunny, equable sweetness had captured my heart, and held it? Now it was as the face of a fiend—a ruthless, unswerving, vengeful fiend. Seeing it thus, I scarcely wondered that this great savage, the chief of a large section of a powerful tribe, should docilely obey its compelling force to the extent of walking forth alone, unarmed, from among his hundreds of turbulent followers, at the behest of one individual, and that individual a woman.

Then as we paced forth in this strange order of march, a spell seemed to have fallen upon all who beheld. Not a hand was raised, not a voice. It was as though they were bewitched. After the first gasp of wonder the silence was intense—awful. But it was not to last.

Chapter Twenty Nine.

Judge and Executioner.

No, it was not to last. Something seemed to break the spell—and that with the same magical suddenness wherewith it had come about. A roar of rage arose, terrible in its menace, thundering upon the stillness of the night. Many had run swiftly back to the huts, and now I could see them, and others, swarming forward, and in the moonlight the glint of assagais. They had returned to arm themselves.

It was a fearful moment. Every nerve within me thrilled, tingled, as revolver gripped, I half-turned my horse, to check, if possible, the onrushing mass. In a moment we should be cut to pieces. We were but two—two against hundreds. Nothing could save us. But Beryl, whose eyes were never removed for so much as a second from her august captive, whose weapon never deflected from straightly covering his form, cried out—

"The first spear thrown means the death of Kuliso!"

Her tones, clear and incisive, rose above the wild, bass hubbub of furious voices. A dead silence succeeded, even as before, and the forward rush became a foot's pace. For they knew that she would keep her word.

Never shall I forget that scene, and assuredly it was one to stand forth in a man's memory for the remainder of his life: the tall form of the savage chieftain stalking sullenly before that pitiless weapon; the resolute, ruthless figure of that beautiful yet terrific avenger of blood, sitting erect as she paced her horse forward with firm, controlling hand, and I, half turned in my saddle, with pistol pointed at the following-on crowd of exasperated barbarians.

This seemed effective, and they paused somewhat. Whether it was that they feared for Kuliso or themselves, or both, they forbore to rush us, and thus, with the crowd still following, but at a respectful distance, we gained the high "neck," beyond which lay our own valley.

And now, behind us, a weird, low, long-drawn cry arose. It seemed to float along the midnight veldt, caught up, echoed forth, from point to point. Was it a rallying cry? If so the whole location would be aroused and upon us, and—what then? Yet at that moment my mind held but two thoughts— admiration for the intrepidity which had prompted and carried out this undertaking; the other the sense of a compelling force which was stronger than myself—that force, Beryl.

"Oh, keep straight on, Kuliso," said the latter. "Do not stop, do not turn your head, or my bullet is certain to crash through the back of it. You know I never miss."

The chief muttered savagely to himself, but he dared not disobey. Then he said—

"Has not our walk lasted long enough, *Umlungase*? Because, if so, I would prefer to return home."

"There are two who will never return home, Kuliso. Soon there will be three," came the answer.

"*Hau!* This is very dark talking—too dark. I know not what is meant."

"You are a liar, Kuliso," replied Beryl calmly. "A great chief of the House of Ndhlambe is a great liar. Ha! Do not stop. Again I warn you—do not stop."

I thought that moment was Kuliso's last. That terrible merciless look, which had temporarily frozen down, gleamed forth anew on Beryl's face. I caught my breath. But again the instinct of self-preservation was stronger than his natural exasperation, and he stepped forward with renewed alacrity.

"We shall never get him in to Fort Lamport, or anything like as far," I said, as the road thither lay but a short space in front of us. "He'll be rescued, or give us the slip long before."

"I don't intend to take him to Fort Lamport, or anything like as far," she answered shortly.

"But—where then?" I asked, thoroughly mystified.

"I am going to take him to look upon those he has murdered. Then I am going to shoot him dead—there, at the place where he has murdered them."

I gasped.

"Great heavens, Beryl! you are never going to do anything so mad!"

"I am. What do you suppose I brought him all this way for—Be careful, Kuliso," relapsing into Kafir. "My eyes are on you, although I'm talking. The bullet, too, is just as ready."

To say that I was thunderstruck is to put it mildly. When I had agreed to our daring and desperate scheme, the arrest of the chief in the very thick of his own followers, I had never bargained for this. The idea was that by seizing him ourselves we could bring him to justice and thus prevent his escape, for if his said arrest were attempted in the ordinary way his followers would never give him up. They would resist any attempt to take him by force, as sure as such attempt were made. This would probably bring on a war, but not condign punishment upon Kuliso. I was filled with admiration for the promptitude and resolution with which she had forced him to accompany us, but that he was marching to his swift and certain doom had never entered my head—that Beryl had constituted herself his judge, jury and executioner, least of all. No, assuredly I had never bargained for this.

"Think better of it," I urged. "Think better of it, and let us carry out our original plan and take him into the town."

"It was never *my* original plan," she answered, in the same low, monotonous tone. "Besides, to use your own words, we should never get him anything like as far. He'd be rescued or give us the slip long before. No. My original plan is the one I am going to carry out—Cross the road, Kuliso. That's right. Keep straight on."

"Beryl, you cannot do this thing yourself," I urged earnestly. "We will manage to keep possession of him somehow, but—leave the rest to the hangman."

"The hangman would never get him, in that case. The Government itself would find some pretext for letting him go, for fear of bringing on a war. Kenrick, you stood beside me when we found *them*—you, too, saw them. Have you so soon forgotten?"

"Forgotten? It would take more than a lifetime to forget that. Still, for your own sake do not do this. I believe you yourself will regret it afterwards. And then the law may call it murder. What then?"

"There isn't a jury in the land that would convict me," she said. "They would call it an act of justice. And it will be. I have thought it all out, you see."

What was I to answer? She was very likely right in her surmise. I remembered Brian's words, uttered the day after my arrival here—words to that very effect.

"Even then it will wear an ugly look," I persisted. "We bring this man a considerable distance across country—the two of us—then shoot him in cold blood."

"Has your blood cooled then, Kenrick?" she said. "Mine hasn't, nor will it, until I see this murderer lying dead beside those he has killed."

"Understand, I am not pleading for his life," I went on, "only that you should not be his executioner. Besides, what if he is the wrong man? What if he should be speaking the truth after all when he says he knows nothing about it?"

"A chief is responsible for the acts of his followers, even under their own law. And he was not speaking the truth; he was lying. I know these people better than you do, Kenrick. If he knew nothing of—of—what has happened, do you think I could have frightened him into going with us? Not for a moment. He knew all about it, and encouraged it, if he did not actually instigate it. He is the principal murderer; afterwards I shall find out the others."

"I was wrong in something I said just now," she went on while I was thinking what next to urge. "I told you I had thought the matter all out. Well, I was wrong. There was one side of it that escaped me."

"And that is?" I said eagerly, catching at a possible straw.

"Yourself."

"Me?"

"Yes. I don't want you to suffer for this in any way. You have helped me this far, Kenrick. Now go—and leave the rest to me. You are not supposed to know what I am about to do; and I'll take care it shall never leak out that you did. Go back to the house and wait for me."

"That's so likely, isn't it?" I answered. "Of course, under any circumstances I'd be sure to slink off and leave you in the middle of the veldt at night, surrounded by Kuliso's cut-throats, watching an opportunity to revenge the death of their chief. That would be me all over, wouldn't it?"

"If only I could see some way out of it—for you! Let me think."

"No, Beryl. Don't think. There's nothing further to be said. Whatever this is we are in it together."

It must not be supposed that during all this talk Beryl's vigilance over her captive was relaxed for one single moment. Nor must it be supposed that I—that either of us—imagined that we were going to have things all our own way, and that Kuliso's people had tamely left their chief to his fate.

We could not see them, but that they were keeping us under observation the whole way neither of us had a shadow of a doubt. But while keeping a sharp look-out, I was able to turn over the situation in my mind. If only Brian had been here. As it was, would he not hold me responsible for Beryl's action, and any disastrous consequences which might ensue? Well, for that matter he could hardly do so, if only that he knew his sister well enough to know also that under the circumstances she would simply laugh at the advice or attempted control of anybody, and that had I discountenanced her project by refusing to accompany her she would simply have embarked on it alone, and then—putting the question on its lowest ground—what sort of figure should I have cut?

Now we were drawing near the fatal spot. We seemed to be moving in a dream—worse—a nightmare. The face of the murdered boy, swollen and ghastly, staring upward to the full broad moon, again seemed to come before my gaze—and that other face, calm, placid, as overtaken by death before a last moment of fleeting horror had had time to stamp it. My nerves were strung to the utmost tension. The Ndhlambe chief would now guess why he had been brought here, and that moment would be his last; for, thus rendered desperate, would he not make one last effort for life? All was still—still as death, save for the tread of the horses; yet momentarily I awaited the roar of the shot which should send Kuliso into that unseen world whither his victims had preceded him.

Then just what I had expected came to pass. Suddenly, and by a rapid, serpentine movement, the chief flung himself down, wriggling for the shade of a thick clump of bush we were passing, and simultaneously dark, sinuous forms started up in front, around us, seeming to spring from nowhere. Beryl's pistol cracked, and then I saw a huge savage—naked, ochre-stained—poising a heavy knobkerrie for a throw. He could not, at that short distance, miss his mark—and that mark, Beryl. And he was behind her, and—she did not see him. It was all done in a second. I drove the spurs home, standing up in the stirrups to catch or ward off the murderous club as, with a whizz, it left his hand. I felt a sharp, fiery dig in the side, in my ears a jarring, roaring crash. My sight was scorched as with the blaze of a million fires, and then— blankness—oblivion!

Chapter Thirty.

"At Last!"

"Hush. Don't talk yet. It's too soon."

A cool hand was laid upon my forehead, while another smoothed the pillows. Bending over me was the face that had been with me in the life for months—in imagination through all the unnameable horrors of my delirium. The large eyes were infinitely tender now, the serene face soft and pitiful.

"It was only my delirium then? It was not true, not real?"

But as I gasped out the question, for I was very weak, my glance lighted on the black heaviness of Beryl's attire. Then I knew that it was true.

"Don't talk any more or you will never get well. And you have got to get well."

"And then you will leave me. I don't want to get well."

"I haven't left you all these weeks, Kenrick, so am not likely to begin now," she answered. "But if you don't obey orders I will. So be quiet."

This was irrefutable; besides, there was that in the sight of her, in her words, in her tones, which shed over me a kind of drowsy peace. I lay still, content to watch her as she sat by my bed doing some needlework, not forgetting every now and then, with watchful care, to brush away the flies that threatened to disturb me. Strange to say, I seemed to feel no curiosity as to the extent of my injuries, or as to what had happened, or even where I was. Her presence was all-sufficient, and soon I dropped off to sleep again.

I pass over the days of convalescence, the recollection of which is somewhat confused. Beryl was seldom absent from my bedside, and I retain a sort of consciousness of others stealing in to look at me. But on such occasions I feigned sleep. I didn't want to see anybody else—anybody but her.

One morning I opened my eyes, feeling strangely well. The object of my unvarying first glance was not there. Her accustomed seat was occupied by Brian.

"Feel better, old chap?" he said, coming over to me. "That's right. Pentridge said you'd take a sudden turn."

"Pentridge? Oh, he's been herding me then? But—Brian—where am I?" For almost for the first time I realised the strangeness of my surroundings.

"Why, you're where you've been the last few weeks—at Fort Lamport—in the new cottage hospital. Pentridge wanted to turn out of his house, and put us all in there, but he'd only just got into it himself, and it's all at sixes and sevens."

The mention of Pentridge seemed to bring back all the old bitterness, and I lay still, not caring to talk any more. But Brian was not of the same mind.

"Do you know, Kenrick, again you have been a sort of Providence to us," he said. "But for you, Beryl would have been killed stone dead—if you hadn't stopped that kerrie. Nothing could have saved her. I saw it."

"You saw it? No, I don't quite follow."

Then he told me what had happened. Old Dumela, fearful for our safety, had warned the neighbours, and had in process of doing so met Brian himself, returning home sooner than was expected. Further, by a piece of great good fortune, a patrol of Mounted Police was making its round, and, joining bands, they had come up in the very nick of time. There would have been nothing left of either of us a minute later, he declared. But that sudden move of mine had saved Beryl. I had received the weapon intended for her.

Well, I knew this of course, but was not aware that she did. Now her care for me stood explained. Its motive was gratitude, and I—well, I had been allowing a sweet new hope to take possession of my mind while I had been lying there, helpless and tended by her, the sight of her gladdening my eyes.

Then Brian went on to tell me the sequel to that fearful night. No one but myself had been seriously injured in the scrimmage. The quickness and unexpected manner of the move made by Kuliso had saved the chief's life, although by a hair's breadth, for the bullet from Beryl's pistol had passed so close to his head as nearly to stun him by the concussion. He had been arrested, but discharged on the insufficiency of evidence connecting him with the murder; but his arrest had produced this amount of good, that his people, anxious for the safety of their chief, had given away the actual murderers, and these proved to be Sibuko, Maqala and one other, who were now awaiting trial.

Not for nothing, then, had my suspicions been aroused by the sight of these two scoundrels hanging about the place, and now I told Brian about it. He sighed.

"Yes," he said. "It's the first and only time I knew the dear old dad commit a serious error of judgment, and heavily he's paid for it. By the way, the double funeral came off here—and was hugely attended. All the world seemed to have rolled up. Do you know, Kenrick, I can hardly stick it on the farm now. You've no idea what it's like without him."

He broke off. And then for some minutes we two grown men were simply not able to speak.

"It's a fortunate thing Beryl did not succeed in shooting that villain Kuliso," he said at last. "Not that he didn't richly deserve it, but—I don't like to think what the result might have been. The law is a very hard-and-fast customer to deal with."

"Yes. I pointed that out to her at the time. But what could I do?"

"Nothing—simply nothing. If I had been there I might have done very much the same sort of thing as she did."

"What's this? Our patient seems to have taken a jump forward," said Pentridge, entering at that moment. "Not been making him talk a lot, have you, Brian?"

"No fear. I've been doing all the talking," was the answer. "Only telling him about things."

"Let me congratulate you, Holt, on the abnormal thickness of your skull," laughed Pentridge. "Otherwise a shattered egg-shell would have been the word instead of a tidy bout of brain fever, not to mention a well-delivered assegai jab beneath the fifth rib."

"You seem to have patched me up, though, to some purpose," I said. And after a few cheery remarks he left me, with a parting injunction to Brian not to let me talk.

But after that I made no more "jumps forward." On the contrary, I was going back. I grew listless and seemed to feel no interest in anything, and my prevailing thought was that it was a pity I had returned to life at all. I even expostulated with Beryl for her attention to me. Pentridge was puzzled.

"I can't make it out at all," I overheard him say one day during a whispered conversation with Beryl. "We ought to have had him on his legs again by now; but he seems determined to cheat me, and that in the wrong direction. Has he anything on his mind, do you know, Miss Matterson?"

"Well, in point of fact, I think he has," she answered with some hesitation. "Of a business nature, he gave me to understand. Of course, I am telling you this in strict confidence, and only then because it might be a guide to you in the treatment of his case."

"Ah! Now I wonder if it would do him any good if he were allowed to see his letters."

"It might."

"All right. Let him have them when he wakes. May do him good, and nothing can do him more harm than brooding over an idea. Good-bye."

I lay with my eyes closed for some time after Pentridge had gone out, thinking over the irony of the situation; for I called to mind our conversation in the garden, and how the position was now exactly that which I had laughingly conjured up. Then I pretended to wake.

"Would you like to see your letters, Kenrick? The doctor says you may now."

I yawned.

"Very kind of him. I don't suppose they're worth the trouble. If there's anything of importance in them it's sure to be bad news or worse. Well, let's have them, Beryl."

There were three, somewhat old as to date. Two were of no importance; but the third! As I glanced dizzily through it, my head swam and the blood rushed to my face, for I was still weak. I dropped back on the pillows.

"Read it, Beryl," I gasped. "Read it for me—for I can't see. Read every word, date and all."

She glanced at me anxiously. Then, rightly judging that it would be better to comply than keep me in a state of agonising suspense, she read it.

Then I, drinking in every word, was hardly able to believe my ears, for the letter was from my agents and expressive of great regret for any inconvenience and anxiety to which their former communication might have put me. They could not conceive how such a mistake could have occurred, but the fact was the funds by some error had not been paid in to the defaulting firm, though only just in time had this course been avoided. Consequently they themselves now held the sum in question awaiting my disposal, and begged to remain, etc., etc.

My little all was saved!

"Read it again, Beryl. Read it again. And be particular as to dates."

She obeyed, and even while she did so her hand dropped upon mine as it lay on the counterpane.

"Oh, Kenrick, I am so glad. I can't tell you how glad I am. Only, remember, my instinct was a true one. Did I not tell you how everything would come right?"

"Yes. But it hasn't. I mean not for me."

"How? Instead of being ruined, as you thought, you are just where you were before. Isn't that coming right?"

"No. I want a great deal more than that. I want—you."

I was looking her straight in the face. A flush came into it, and there was the sweetest, tenderest glow in her eyes. It seemed that the hand which rested in mine returned the pressure.

"Beryl—darling—my love for you has been steadily growing since we first became inmates of the same house. I was on the point of telling you so when that idiot Trask came clattering in upon us that day we were riding back from Stacey's. Then, afterwards, as you know, there were other things that made the time not an opportune one; and the day before you returned home I got the news that made me think I was a beggar."

"Yes. And you took to behaving very strangely towards me then, as I think I told you."

"Shall I tell you something, dearest? I was beastly jealous of Pentridge."

"Were you? Well, you needn't be ever again. Shall I tell *you* something, dearest—only as a secret? He asked me to marry him."

"The day he left?"

She nodded.

"I thought he would," I said. "And—why didn't you?"

"Because I greatly preferred some one else."

"Who is the 'some one else'?"

"If you will promise not to talk any more—you have already talked a great deal too much—I'll tell you. You will? Well, then—" and the look upon her face was to my eyes simply heavenly, as she bent down her sweet lips to my ear, touched it with them, and whispered just one word: "You."

I hardly know what the next few moments contained, except that it was far too radiantly blissful to put into mere words. Then looking down upon me, her cool hand lovingly moving over my forehead and temples, she said—

"Now you will be quick and get well—for my sake, won't you, Kenrick dear?"
"Rather! Pentridge may consider the cure complete. My mind is clear now, at any rate." And then I stopped, feeling rather ashamed of my exhilaration and happiness, considering how recent was the blow which had fallen, and said so. But she reassured me.

"It is just as the dear old dad would have wished," she said. "He had such an opinion of you, Kenrick. Now—where is your promise? You were not to talk any more, do you remember?"
"But I have hardly said anything yet. And—I want to."
"Haven't you? You have been delirious, remember, dearest, and when people are delirious they say a great deal." And with a glad, mischievous laugh, again she bent down her lips to mine.

I gained strength daily now, almost hourly. But Pentridge wondered not at the sudden change when he learned how it had been brought about. He congratulated us in a cordial, manly way, poor chap. Yes, he was a fine fellow, was Pentridge.

We had a sad and painful time of it, Beryl and I, at the trial of the three murderers, for we had to give evidence, and that meant a re-opening of the old wounds. But Sibuko and Maqala and the other Kafir were sentenced to be hanged; and hanged they were, in the gaol at Fort Lamport, a couple of weeks or so afterwards. With their richly-deserved fate the vendetta which culminated in this last tragedy was closed; for Kuliso, strange to say, conceived such a vast admiration and respect for Beryl's magnificent intrepidity on that fatal night, that he made it known among his tribesmen that all further acts of hostility or molestation towards us, of any kind, were to cease; and as he still emphatically disclaimed any knowledge of or complicity in the sad tragedy, we gave him the benefit of the doubt, and dwelt side by side, at any rate on neighbourly terms.

For after Beryl and I were married—quietly, by reason of what had gone before—as Brian showed not the smallest intention of following our example, we continued to make our home at Gonya's Kloof, and our partnership in farming concerns prospered exceedingly, and in our home circle we were as happy as the still lingering shadow of bereavement would allow us to be. And it was a shadow. Poor little George! We missed his merry impudence a good many times a day, and as for the wise, kind father and friend—why, for long the recollection of him was blank indeed; and long it was before Time even began to heal the wound which that recollection had left.

Well, that is my story. I don't know that it is much of a story, but it's a true one, and that I, Kenrick Holt, should ever have been brought to write a story at all seems passing strange, most of all to myself; indeed, I never should have, had it not been for a friend of mine who used to come and stay at our place, and shoot. He was always keen on reminiscences—if local and tragic all the better—and my own romance appealed to him to such an extent that he was continually urging me to turn it into a book; which was sporting of him, for he was very much in the book-writing line himself—especially with reference to my now adopted country—and might easily have used it himself, turning it to account on behalf of his own pocket. However, he was too much of a sportsman for that, so—here it is.

Finis.

Milton Keynes UK
Ingram Content Group UK Ltd.
UKHW042145281024
450365UK00010B/624